COUTURE

The Great Designers

MARCH 1970 HARPER'S

BAZAAR

WHAT'S
GOING
FOR YOU

FROM
AMERICA
PARIS

ELLE

Comment choisir
re

FASHION FOR MEN/SUMMER $1.50

GQ
GENTLEMEN'S QUARTERLY

LIVING
FIRST
CLASS

Queen

VOGUE

ITALIA

TOGRAFATA
AVEDON
LTA MODA
PARIGI

ABITI
NTI DA
PRARE
ITO

EZZA
OVO CORPO
A DONNA D'OGGI

EDWARD HEATH
ON BRITAIN IN THE 70s

HarpeRS
& Queen

$2/00

ANTHONY HADEN-G
and THE CASE
OF THE DARK LAD

MAY 1973 • 35p

YOUR MONEY
AND YOUR LIFE:
How to convert
salary into capital·
How to invest

SAINT LAURENT
rive gauche

© 2005 Assouline Publishing, Inc.

601 West 26th Street, 18th Floor
New York, NY 10001, USA
Tel: 212-989-6810 Fax: 212-647-0005
www.assouline.com

ISBN: 2 84323 576 6

Color separation by Gravor (Switzerland)
Printed by GraficheMilani (Italy)

LYNN
FRONT TO BACK

For Mark and Sam

turnin' the pages in this old book
seems familiar
might be worth a second look

someday you'll find what you're lookin' for
someday you'll find everything you're looking for
someday you'll find everything you're looking for
someday you'll find everything you're looking for, yeah

Neil Young

Excerpts from
"Bandit"
Greendale Album

FOREWORD

A picture tells a thousand words. This is the story of my girlfriend Lynn Kohlman, a woman of style, one who creates fashion just in her being. This is the journey of a woman whose extraordinary story is an inspiration, constantly searching for the meaning of life and its beauty—inside and out.

As a model and a photographer, Lynn has lived on both sides of the camera. To know Lynn is to know a woman who lives life to the fullest. She loves challenges of all kinds, using her extraordinary focus to figure out the best approach to take. She observes, she witnesses, she explores, she analyzes, and she gives it her all—as a wife, a mother, a friend, a photographer, a model, a yogi or as a woman facing cancer. It is not a coincidence that Lynn chose photography, which captures a moment and lets it live forever.

One of my best friends, Lynn and I have been together for every important moment of our adult lives. Personally and professionally, we share a history and have helped shape each other's future. I met Lynn when she came to model for my first ad campaign at Anne Klein. She was a superstar, famous as the fresh face of Perry Ellis. I asked her to look hard, driving, and sexy. My husband Stephan, who designed the stage set, took one look at her and said, "Who is that bitch?"

Soon afterwards, I convinced Lynn to attend EST with me. You can't do EST with someone without becoming close, and Lynn and I became very close. Along the way, Lynn stopped modeling and started photographing. When I introduced Anne Klein II, I asked Lynn to do our ads and catalog. She nailed it. Years later, when we were opening DKNY, I needed someone to be my voice and support at DKNY and to work with Jane Chung, the Executive Vice President of Design. Once again, I called Lynn, who styled the clothes with her androgynous street edge.

Our friendship only deepened. Stephan loved Lynn. He and I had become a foursome with Lynn and her husband Mark, hanging out at the beach in the summer and taking ski trips in the winter. Sometimes Lynn and I went without the guys. Lynn and my daughter Gabby had become fellow adventurers and went on a rafting trip above the Arctic Circle and, during another summer, went on a whitewater river journey in British Columbia. Lynn's son Sam and my granddaughter Mackenzie, who are a year apart, became thick as thieves. Everywhere Lynn and I turned, our lives intersected. Lynn was still photographing for me, only this time it was pictures of my family. She has captured my most treasured portraits of my daughter, my grandchildren, and, of course, Stephan—including the one that appeared everywhere when he passed away.

Lynn and I continue to seek enlightenment wherever it takes us. This quest culminated in me introducing yoga to Lynn. You have to understand, Lynn is Joe Jock, so yoga was not her first choice. I took Lynn to Parrot Cay to meet Rodney Yee and Colleen Saidman. Lynn instantly mastered poses that took me years to conquer. Her affinity for yoga was mind blowing. And, it turned out, fortuitous, too: shortly afterwards, Lynn discovered she had breast cancer. (Only Lynn could run into an old friend who just happened to be a psychic and told her to check her breast.) Throughout Lynn's medical ordeal, yoga has been one of her emotional salvations.

Cancer is a journey I know too much about. It has always been prevalent in my life. Anne Klein had breast cancer and Stephan had lung cancer. Lynn had been there for Stephan and there was no question I'd be there for her. I helped Lynn find specialists and stayed at her side through surgery. It was during another yoga trip to Parrot Cay that an unrelated cancer appeared in Lynn's brain (Rodney and I thought she was experiencing Kundalini rising, but no, it was a seizure). We flew home. I was all set to cancel the elective surgery I had scheduled, but Lynn stopped me: Can I photograph it, she asked? My surgery was literally a day before hers. Lynn's photos are amazing, simply beyond—but stored away in a locked cabinet. After Lynn's surgery, she begged me to let a photographer capture our mutual recoveries—those photos you can see here. Together Lynn and I healed, a bit scarred from the journey, but still intact.

Serious as life gets, Lynn likes to laugh. A lot. Even during her darkest moments, Lynn maintains her humor, like the time a punker asked who did her cool hair-and-staples look and she responded "Dr. Holland at Sloan-Kettering." Lynn is the ultimate study in contrasts: feminine and masculine, powerful and vulnerable, a city woman and an outdoor adventurer, incredibly warm and extremely cool.

Lynn is one of the strongest people I know, as well as one of the most sensitive. Lynn's passion for life inspires me every day—now more than ever. Only a formidable spirit like Lynn could embrace the darkness and find such inspiring light. It's an honor to call her my friend.

Donna Karan

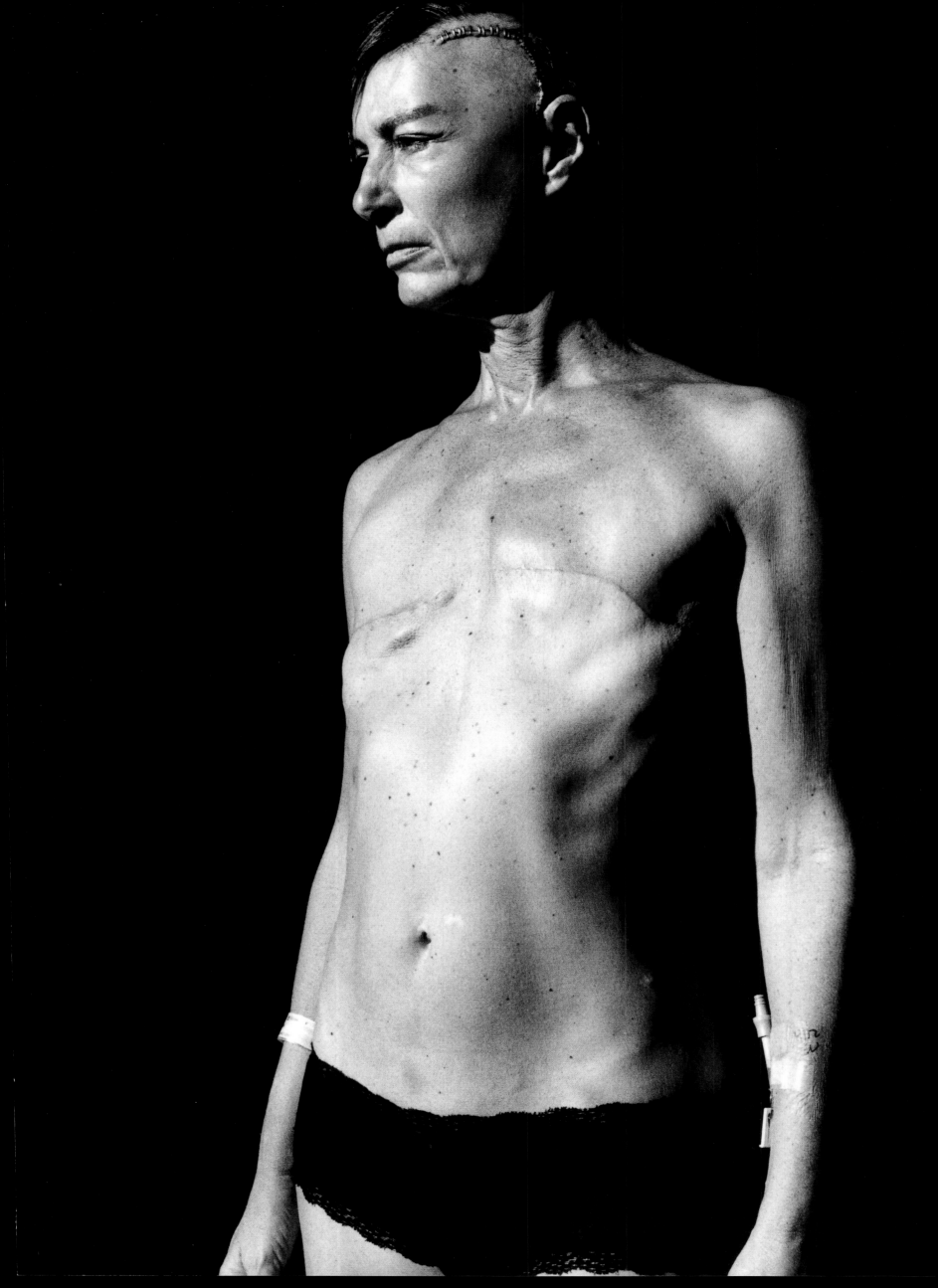

INTRODUCTION

Having death as my constant companion has changed my life. Within a matter of seven months, I went from being healthy and whole to missing two breasts and having 37 titanium staples in my head. I needed to find my own inner source of strength and power. Maybe other people don't have to go through cataclysmic transformations for this kind of awakening to take place, but for me, that's what happened.

In some ways, it seems as if everything has just fallen into my lap—modeling, photography, adventures in the wilderness, even cancer. But has it really? Perhaps I've chosen these paths. Either way, it has been up to me to decide how to respond. As random and unconnected as they may seem, the experiences of the past four decades have been vital preparation for confronting the enormous challenge facing me now. I had always envisioned my various careers and interests as disparate cords, but now I see them intertwined, a rope that I can hold onto, a lifeline as I battle cancer.

Of all the chapters in my life, the one I find hardest to revisit is my modeling career. For one thing, it began more than 35 years ago. For another, I was always a little ashamed and embarrassed by it. Here I was, graduating from Oberlin College, with an Art History major, summa cum laude, Phi Beta Kappa, and this was the path I picked? I had never worn makeup and was totally uninterested in fashion magazines. And most importantly, I'd always thought of myself as a timid person. When I had my first photos taken, it seemed an impossible task to cut through my insecurities. I had no sense of my own beauty, and modeling didn't change that.

It remains mysterious to me why I went to modeling agencies to be interviewed. Certainly, being rejected by Eileen Ford of Ford Models didn't make me feel any better about myself. She said I was too "eccentric" looking, but she would reconsider me after a nose job! The other renowned agent, Wilhelmina, took me on immediately and sent me out to get "tested" by a few up-and-coming photographers in order to build my portfolio.

One of my earliest modeling jobs was for *The New York Times Magazine*. Rather than taking place in a photo studio with artificial lighting and white no-seam paper for a backdrop, which was standard operating procedure back then, this shoot was outdoors in the country. I was seated on the grass in front of a great old barn. I could feel the wind, smell the fresh-cut hay—I was a peasant, it was real. In previous test shoots, I'd never been certain what I was supposed to do with my face or my body. Sometimes the photographer would play music and expect me to dance around or say things to try to elicit an expression, but it all seemed awkward to me, as I didn't have the confidence or attitude that a lot of models have. But here, in nature, I felt completely at ease. I *could* do this!

Because I wasn't interested in the usual perks of modeling—money, travel, fame—I had to find another reason to justify it to myself. I also realized from the start that modeling was not a long-term career, and unless I became a model-turned-actress or married rich (as many models do), I'd better think about my next move. I quickly became drawn to photography; with my background in Art History, it seemed an obvious path. Photographers thrilled me with their originality and style. I decided to get an on-the-job "masters degree."

One of my initial tests was with Arthur Elgort, who was then assisting Gösta Peterson. At the end of one photo session, Arthur and I went back to his apartment where, after processing the negatives, he developed the pictures in his bathroom. He had three trays arranged in the bathtub, and once the print was fully "cooked," he handed it to me and I rinsed it by flushing it in the toilet. Then he hung it on a clothesline strung across his bathtub to drip dry, like stockings. This was my first lesson.

Thanks to modeling, I had the opportunity to "study" with many of the great photography "professors" of the time, including my icon, Irving Penn. One day I was working with Mr. Penn (you weren't allowed to call him Irving or Irv). He disappeared downstairs to his darkroom, as he often did, giving the makeup artist and the hairdresser time to open the window wide and have a cigarette, and for me to take a closer look—much closer—at his lighting setup. He came back into the room without my noticing. I felt like a little child who was discovered cheating by the teacher! Instead of being annoyed, he sat me down and began to sketch the setup for me to keep. (I asked for an autograph, but judging from his expression, I think that I was pushing it too far!)

I was shocked and thrilled that he was drawing this just for me. He looked at me, and in response to my expression said that he could not even count the number of assistants who had come through his doors. Each of them had learned all of his lighting techniques intimately. Not one had become an Irving Penn!

London in the '70s was the perfect place for me. I didn't have the wholesome, corn-fed look that most American editors and advertisers were looking for, but in Europe I was an instant sensation. The "London Style"—edgy, punk, androgynous—suited me and allowed my strong personal style to blossom. This was reflected in my self-confidence, which improved dramatically. Once a bookworm from Teaneck, New Jersey, I was now a "hot commodity!"

In addition to photographers, modeling exposed me to all the top fashion designers of the day: Zandra Rhodes, Ozzie Clark, Bill Gibb, and particularly, Yves Saint Laurent. I also became close friends with the rising stars Kenzo and the Argentinean duo Pablo and Delia. To my mind, they were as creative as the photographers: gifted with their "artists' hands." It was easy to see fashion design as another creative field to study while modeling.

Although I'd been modeling primarily for European designers, one day Perry Ellis called me in for a "go-see." As soon as we met, we fell in love with each other—or at least I fell in love with him. He fell in love with my offbeat, sporty style. At the time, almost everything I wore was vintage. When I went to meet Perry in New York, I had on an oversize white linen men's pants suit I'd picked up in London. The pants were wrapped around me and held up with a belt, and the jacket was simply huge. We went out to dinner at Raoul's, down in SoHo, and he asked me to collaborate with him. I thought of myself as his muse, but he gave me the title "assistant designer." I had plenty of style, but knew almost zero about designing and couldn't draw for the life of me.

Perry did a whole show based on that white linen suit, in which everything was oversized. I modeled for him on the runway and worked on his collections with him and his talented head designer, Patricia Pastor, for the next several years. Meanwhile, I continued to model in Europe, where my career was at its peak. Finally, as the '80s approached, I realized that my time as a model was drawing to an end. It was the final fitting for one of Perry's shows, I rolled myself into the studio in a rented wheelchair. Perry looked at me, and all of the color drained out of his face. I'm not sure whether he was more worried about my health or the fact that I wouldn't be able to do his show the next day! I told him to relax, that I'd practiced "wheelchair modeling," and then proceeded to roll down the runway, full of attitude, even doing a daring spin at the end. He was not amused, but he got my point: it was time for me to move on.

As much as Perry valued my fashion skills, he encouraged me to take my photography seriously and to pursue it professionally. After all, I had been "studying" for a decade, soaking up as much knowledge as I could. I felt strongly that while hiding under the wings of a designer was creative and fun, it didn't hold the visibility or responsibility of being out there on my own. I had to overcome tremendous fears to take on this new challenge, to exercise my own "artist's hand" and be judged on my own merits. That's why it was the path I had to choose. After years of being on one side of the lens, I needed to be on the other. Front to back.

To build up my portfolio, I photographed male models from Zoli Agency, which had been my agent in New York. Zoli was known for having the best male models in town. I preferred photographing men, then I didn't have to deal with hair and makeup people breathing down my neck. It turned out to be a great career move, as there were no other female photographers, that I remember, shooting only male models. Even though people assumed my reason was sexual, it wasn't—but let me say, it didn't hurt one bit!

Constantly practicing photography taught me an unexpected lesson—it was portraiture that grabbed my heart and soul. Each time, no matter how full-length I began, as I gained courage, I would creep up on my subject until I was peering directly into his eyes as he gazed directly back. I could feel my timid nature dissipate as the clicks of my Nikon got smoother and smoother. My subject and I would then start to "dance" as I moved slowly from side to side, up and down, like doing Tai Chi. Focused so completely, everything would become quiet and peaceful, until it was impossible to separate the observer from the observed. At this moment, I knew I'd captured the photo. The feeling was total elation—like flying. This experience was so explosive that years later, when faced with cancer, I knew that accessing this place within me would give me the strength to fight for my life.

I quickly came to the attention of Andy Warhol, whose *Interview* magazine was the place for portrait photographers. One day I got a call from Robert Hayes, the managing editor, saying that Andy would like to see my portfolio. I thought for a moment—*what* portfolio? I thought quickly and said my book was tied up at a client's for the next few days. Then I dashed to the nearest art supply store, bought a portfolio, ran back to the darkroom, and worked day and night to produce finished prints. Two days later, I brought them to The Factory. Thank goodness I didn't meet Andy at that time—I was far too flustered. Robert took my portfolio and, I assume, showed it to Andy, for I was hired to work the very next day and every month for some time thereafter.

One month, I was assigned to shoot Joe Theismann, then the quarterback of the Washington Redskins. I was shown to the "photo dugout," where I was the only woman, the only one with a Nikon, and the only one who wasn't in foul-weather gear. For some reason, Theismann decided he didn't want me to see his face. No problem—I figured I'd catch him as he went to his bench or at the Gatorade stand. It didn't turn out quite like that. Soon it was pouring and everything became a mud bath. As I slid up and down the sidelines, I was so intensely focused on Joe that I neglected to notice that both teams were surging in my direction. All the other photographers had abandoned their positions, but I just stood there, completely oblivious to the onslaught, until at the last moment I leaped back and avoided being tackled. I never ended up getting Joe's face, only his back. At least he had a good butt!

With all this editorial exposure, my career as a photographer took off. Perry Ellis gave me my first commercial assignment. Then I worked with Donna Karan, whom I'd gotten to know through modeling, shooting all of her Anne Klein II promotionals and ads.

On July 29, 1986, my son, Sam, was born, bringing my husband, Mark, and I indescribable joy. I continued to shoot and even travel, as long as I was allowed to bring Sam with a nanny. But soon it became clear to me that my attention was divided, and without being able to give photography my all, my pleasure in it decreased. I needed a break.

It didn't take long for Donna to entice me into styling the first fashion show for her DKNY line. In no time at all I became her fashion director and, eventually, creative director. Little did I suspect that for more than the next decade, I had chosen, or maybe not, a path which held so much for me to learn.

I joined Donna virtually from the birth of her business and traveled with her as it grew at an astonishing speed. I even had the honor of standing on the balcony of the New York Stock Exchange as she rang the opening bell and her company became public. I never had been as proud of a friend.

I look back at those years and recognize a profound lesson had been taught to me. She chose a career full of challenges, which she elected to perceive as opportunities to be creative, to really explore who she was and grow. It is now my difficult time, and I have learned from her lead.

It was at Donna's urging that I took up yoga. For a long time I had avoided yoga because it seemed like just another fad. But a few years ago, she convinced me to attend a 5-day retreat with the master teacher, Rodney Yee. It was a revelation, a coming home.

Practicing yoga, focusing intensely on each pose, gave me that same sense of being swept away as photography. On that first retreat, I immediately realized the connection between the two, and intuitively knew the importance this would have later in my life. I was so moved by this experience of yoga that I wanted to capture my intense emotions on film. In yoga, my mind and body unite and touch my soul. Photographing yoga, I had a tremendous desire to express myself more deeply than ever before. I shot portraits of Rodney as he meditated, with his hair softly moving across his face; of the light glancing off his hands in lotus position, so full of energy; and of his feet as they gripped the ground, so much like the roots of a tree reaching out and full of life force.

I have found there is within me a quiet, white space where I am transformed. I tap into my inner peace and strength and out emerges someone new. Whenever and wherever I can create this sensation, that's where I need to be. If there is *anything* that I can do for my cure of cancer this is it. I pursue it with photography, delve into it with yoga and meditation, and explore it in the wilderness.

Photography and the wilderness are always changing, evoking the passage of light, of time. They're both about capturing and living in the moment, about being here now. Every time I pick up my camera, I feel like a beginner, an explorer, just as I do when I set off on a wilderness experience.

I was with family and friends whitewater rafting down the Klinaklini River in Canada. One morning before sunrise, I awakened. It was so quiet I could almost hear it. I stuck my head out of my tent, and knew if there ever was a time and a place to get up and take some photos, this was it. There was a deep fog rolling in from the iceberg increasing my sense of quiet, solitude, and inner peace. Barely emerging through the blue fog were two birds, and ever so faintly I could hear the flapping of their wings.

Of course, I'm not so naive as to believe the wilderness is simply about pretty dawns. Over the years, I've learned that it holds many challenges, which is an essential part of its attraction for me. For years, we celebrated my birthday in August with a whitewater rafting trip: down the Middle Fork, the Main and Lower Salmon, the Snake, the Grand Canyon, the Tatshensheni, the Firth, the Turnagain, and the Klinaklini.

In addition to the physical challenges and the aesthetic rewards, part of what draws me to these places is experiencing nature's raw power. For example, I was warned and trained early on how to survive if I had the misfortune of bumping into a black or grizzly bear. For a black bear, I was instructed to make myself big and noisy; for a grizzly, which you can identify by its long curved nails, I was told to fall into a fetal position.

On my birthday one year, we were rafting the Main Salmon. I chose a magnificent spot to set up my tent: up a hill, surrounded by a circle of Ponderosa Pines, with the campsite visible below. I dropped my dry bag to take a pee, when I heard noises in the very nearby bushes. Up rose a bear. I don't know why I didn't scream for help, but for some reason I was being very rational and doing exactly what I'd been taught: checking its "manicure" for the worst case scenario—a grizzly—and preparing to make myself big if it was a black bear. But what appeared instead was a beautiful honey-colored bear with matching eyes. I had been taught how to respond to black, to brown, but honey never came up! He stared at me almost sweetly, and I returned the gaze by staring directly into his eyes for what seemed like an endless time. At last I was "saved" by the rest of the group clattering up the hill banging pots and pans. All except Donna, that is, who had jumped into a raft armed with a wiffle bat!

The other main danger was capsizing. Since I wore a life jacket and a helmet, I didn't perceive it as life-threatening. If the worst should occur, I was told to keep my feet downstream and, when I saw an eddy, just flip my body over and swim for shore.

Rafting the Klinaklini in British Columbia one time, we approached the top of the first of the class 5 rapids (in Canada, a class 5 rating is the same as a class 10 in the USA). Everyone hiked to an overlook where the guides carefully studied this ferocious white water. It was determined that I would paddle in the first raft along with Mark, two friends, and one guide as our oarsman. Somehow, right at the top, when we'd barely entered what's known as the "tongue," BAM! Over we went. Suffice it to say, there were the usual holes and a long drop with the addition of stacks of logs and sifters (branches of fallen trees that can prevent passage by catching you under water). It was my first experience facing death, and I determined at that moment that drowning was not how I would prefer to go.

Having a near-death experience was still no preparation for the "Big C." It is difficult to find the words to describe how I felt each of the three times I was told I had cancer. The first time, in September 2002, it was my right breast, and I was emotionally numb. The second time, in October 2002, it was my left breast, and I was devastated. The third time, in March 2003, it was my brain, and I felt like I was falling into an unimaginable, endless black abyss.

When I was a very young child, I had nightmares of falling into an abyss. I screamed and my mother came into my room to comfort me. I woke and held on to her. Then my room got longer and longer, like that scene from Alice in Wonderland when she drinks a potion and gets bigger and bigger, and then smaller and smaller, and I held onto my mother even more tightly. My mother passed away on October 7, 2002. Instead, I have the most magnificent man to hold on to, my husband, Mark. He, along with family and friends, has helped me pull myself out of this abyss.

My mother had cancer in her left breast in her fifties and, after a mastectomy, lived another thirty years. So, unlike most women, I didn't have this image of breast cancer as a death sentence, although I was very diligent about yearly checkups. Given my family history, I shouldn't have been completely stunned by my own diagnosis. However, nothing can really prepare you for having the roulette wheel stop on your number.

After it was discovered that I had cancer in both breasts, I needed to decide whether or not to have a double mastectomy. The truth was that my breast surgeon wasn't painting a pretty picture for any other option, but I believed that she felt it would be better for my peace of mind if I felt like the choice was mine. One week after my mother's death, I was back under the knife.

At that time, my oncologist wanted me to consider deeply how I felt about forgiveness and regret. He had no idea that my mother had died a week earlier, but it was immediately where my mind took me.

Forgiveness was easier for me to understand than regret. I had, in a very small way, and far too little, and a lot too late, forgiven my mother just before she passed away. She was suffering from Alzheimer's, but I was reassured that she knew from my embraces how I felt. When I took her portrait that day, so close to her passing, she looked directly into my lens and tried so hard to smile. There were tears in her eyes as I held her fragile and transparent hand. However, there's still one thing I can't forgive her for: just like Mom I have cellulite thighs! Oh well, no miniskirts, no shorts, and no bathing suits without a sarong.

Since then, I've been going around my world forgiving as much as possible. Most importantly, my brother and I needed to forgive each other, big time. I also needed to admit that I'm a very stubborn person, particularly with my husband. But, whether right or wrong, instead of letting things hang over us, I now quickly apologize and forgive. This sure has taken a tremendous load off my shoulders.

Regret gave me pause. Why had my oncologist used this word? Was it so I wouldn't regret chopping off my breasts? Was it so I wouldn't regret the relationships I never had with my mother and father? Then I just happened to read a quote by Mark Twain: "You will be more disappointed by the things you didn't do than by the things you did." This opened my eyes to a whole new perspective. I looked again at the meaning of regret, and instead of backward, I began to look forward. I decided to wake each morning with a smile on my face and love in my heart, determined to have no regrets about the day, to make it as happy and joyous as possible. One day at a time, moment by moment, I was getting lighter.

Back to the "Big C" word—32C, that is. Before my mastectomy, that was my bra size. Now that I would have a choice in the matter, I wanted something a little smaller—somewhere between an A and a B. I also absolutely did not want those perky, pancake-shaped implants; I wanted something more natural looking. My doctor told me there was a "teardrop" implant that would look just like my own breasts. In my imagination, I envisioned waking up the morning after the operation stunned by these beautiful new breasts. Unfortunately, I was not eligible for immediate reconstruction with my own fat tissue, as I didn't have enough to spare. It was the first time I had heard anyone tell me I was too fit! You just can't win.

I was sitting with my doctor as he was explaining about expanders and implants and all I could do was cry. But somehow, through my hysteria, a thought struck me. "Where do you get the nipples?"

"Oh, we get them from between your legs," my doctor casually explained.

"BETWEEN MY LEGS? Whoa! That must hurt! I mean, if you're looking for skin that's about the same color..."

"No, no, no!" he replied quickly. "We don't take it from there. We take it from here." He indicated the top of my inner thigh.

"Oh, good, then can you do liposuction at the same time?" I said, trying to see the glass half full.

"Afraid not," he answered. Then I asked where the color came from.

"We tattoo it, you pick the color yourself."

I imagined a paint strip with all these shades of pink, like from Benjamin Moore. Then another thought intruded: I get waxed down there. "Ah, excuse me, but aren't the nipples going to be a little hairy?"

"They can be," he replied.

In my mind's eye I saw me and Mark in the bathroom together. He's shaving his beard and I'm shaving my nipples! Shocked and speechless, I burst out crying again.

After my double mastectomy, I went to the doctor every week and he put some saline solution into my expanders and blew them up little by little, like balloons, to stretch the skin and muscle tissue. Nobody had warned me how painful expanders could be. It was like medieval torture every week, it was as if the screws were being turned tighter and tighter. I felt like I was in a cage. Now I could relate to Frida Kahlo!

One of my doctors had warned me that breast surgeons always give you larger breasts than you want, so I kept telling him, "No bigger than a B, keep this in your head, B, as in boob!" So one day I went in there and said, "Why am I getting stretched so large? I only want A's or B's."

"You have to expand more than you need so that the tissue can form around the implant," he explained.

"Okay," I replied, "but how big can the implant be? We're talking about a small cup size here."

"Well, let me show it to you." He then brought out what I can only describe as a Dolly Parton size.

"You know I wanted no larger than a B cup!" I cried. He proceeded to tell me that in the teardrop shape, smaller implants are not available in this country. If I wanted an A or a B cup, I could get them in Brazil, Canada, or France, but in the United States they hadn't been approved by the FDA.

Talk about a man's world! "Do you know a doctor in Canada?" I asked him. He demurred. "Well then, get the name of one," I went on. "I'll pick them up and drive them back." I had this image of myself in a black-and-white movie, with my face pressed against the window of my car as a customs officer cuffed my hands behind my back and read me my Miranda rights for the crime of smuggling breast implants across the US border!

As it turned out, I didn't have to worry about how to get hold of smaller implants, because three months after having the expanders put in, I got a major infection. My temperature rose to almost 105 degrees and I was in the hospital on intravenous antibiotics. The expanders had to come out because you can't fully cure an infection that's in a synthetic material in your body. So, I underwent yet another operation.

After the expanders were removed, all I saw were boobs—on TV, in advertising and movie posters, outside on the street. There was a pair of giant boobs staring down at me from a billboard as I entered the Midtown Tunnel. Riding the subway, an ad caught my eye for a breast cancer walk featuring two young, nubile women in tight T-shirts, obviously without bras. I already felt like a guy—I was without breasts, and now all I saw were boobs everywhere!

Just because I no longer had breasts didn't mean I no longer wanted to have sex. But I was thwarted by yet another problem: my incredible shrinking vagina! Something else the doctors neglected to tell me about—do they think that women over the age of fifty have retired from sex? Intercourse became excruciating because my vagina was so much smaller. I had read that it could be a result of menopause, but nobody had bothered to tell me that chemotherapy aggravates the situation. Thank goodness I wasn't too embarrassed to ask what the hell was happening. I was informed that vaginal estrogen pills or diaphragms can restore the elasticity of the vaginal tissue. (Because they're very localized, they're not a threat, even if you have breast cancer.)

A month after the expanders came out, I was at a yoga retreat with Rodney on an island when, taking a nap, I had what I can only describe as an out-of-body experience. It was as if something was running up my spine, and I had this terrible taste in my mouth. Meanwhile, I was watching myself from someplace on the ceiling, looking down, feeling like I would never return to my body. I woke up screaming, shaking uncontrollably. The next day in class, while lying down in shivassana at the end of class, it happened again. This time Rodney, Donna, and everyone else crowded around me. Rodney declared that I was having a kundalini experience. Donna nodded in earnest agreement.

Isn't kundalini what yogis strive for after decades of practice? I thought. How can I be going through kundalini after less than a year of yoga? Then I turned to my dear friend and said, "Donna, I have brain cancer." Donna immediately called a neurologist she knew, who told her to get me on a plane back to New York. If only it had been kundalini.

Even though I knew I had brain cancer, hearing the words from a neurologist was a different story. After surgery, she told me I had Stage IV brain cancer. Ever the good student, I raised my hand. "Is that 4 out of 10?" No, it was 4 out of 4—the worst, most aggressive kind, known as glioblastoma. My doctors had assumed that it was a metastasis from my breast cancer. It was much worse. I had another primary cancer. Now the Grim Reaper was well within sight. I could already feel his chilling presence.

Fortunately, I have a superb array of doctors at Memorial Sloan-Kettering Cancer Center. I believe there are no better. If there is a cure, they will lead me to it. I also recognized that I have to take responsibility for myself, after all, it is my mind and my body. I know how important positive thinking is. I needed to face cancer and death head on. I had been slammed to the ground and thrown down an abyss. Now I envisioned picking myself up and emerging a samurai warrior, sword in hand, ready for battle.

I approached brain cancer as I did every challenge. I pushed and pushed, using all my strength and power. But it didn't work. Two weeks after surgery, the tumor returned to its original size. I was suffering from frequent seizures. Back in the hospital, I was put on a program of intense radiation every morning and chemotherapy every evening. Thinking back on this time, I can see Robert Duvall in *Apocalypse Now*, cigar in mouth, and hear the echo of his voice saying, "I love the smell of napalm in the morning!"

It was difficult to see an upside in all this, but it did hold a lesson for me: I needed to back off from my pushing. It was resulting in the worst thing for someone with cancer: tremendous tension and stress. When I began yoga, I always clenched my jaw in my desire to conquer each pose. I soon learned, however, that if I relaxed my jaw and face, that conquering the pose was not the goal. If I had thought about it, I also knew that a true samurai had to soften and relax enough to both absorb and deflect the energy of the opponent, to use the enemy's strength and power.

I looked at all the skills I have in my repertoire to be that warrior, to really come to terms with cancer, to deflect its attack. Decades of experience in meeting and conquering challenges have left me well-equipped. My rope is strong.

I already have western science covering me, and so, as in a battle, I needed to come in from the east. Whether I am on chemotherapy or not, I am on a concentrated regime of meditation and yoga to focus my breath and grab my soul; acupuncture and craniosacral therapy to normalize the flow of my energy as it courses through my body. My routine also includes a raw foods diet to feed my body and soul (alas, no more burgers and fries—well, not quite true!); spinning like a whirling dervish to increase my heart rate and release endorphins; listening to music—especially Neil Young; body sculpting because I hate having chicken wings as arms; humor because I need to laugh; and visualization just because it's fun.

My craniosacral therapist was the one who planted the idea of visualization in my head. She suggested I "see" something or someone small enough to be in my head, working on my tumor. Someone small, I thought: a dwarf! Even better, how about seven? The Seven Dwarfs! Every day, all except Doc, who acts as lookout, they enter into my top chakra (the very top of my skull), and climb down a rope ladder with all their equipment—wheelbarrows, buckets, pickaxes—singing, "Hi-ho, hi-ho, it's off to work we go!" Then they go to work, chipping away at the tumor, tossing it into their wheelbarrows, filling their buckets, climbing the ladder, then passing it up to Doc. He tosses it up into the air, where it evaporates into gold fairy dust. Day after day, they are my constant companions, and the tumor shrinks.

My other visualization, Lance Armstrong, accompanies me to all my spinning classes. He sits or lies down in front of my bike and pushes me harder, as if I were going to be one of his teammates in the Tour de France. I read in his book that to fool his opponents he smiles and looks as if it's easy. I follow Lance's trick, although spinning has never been easy for me. I think I'm the only one in the spinning room with a smile plastered across my face. The instructor must think I'm a grinning idiot, but I'm the one who finds that smiling *does* make it easier!

Smiling—what a miracle. Years ago, there was an article on the front page of the Science section of the *New York Times* that discussed the chemicals released by smiling and their positive impact on both mind and body. I find myself smiling a lot now, to the point where sometimes my mouth hurts. Walking down the street, I'll be smiling and strangers will smile back. I've become a smile ambassador!

Smiling is a powerful weapon. Each morning I wake up happy. I try to keep my smile going all day. Not all the time, of course. When I'm taking chemo and puking all night, or am frustrated by the unimaginable fatigue brought on by my daily antiseizure medications, I'm not exactly going, "How great!"

It's ironic, however, that cancer has been an unexpected gift that has brought with it dramatic change and transformation. I look back and embrace the decades of my life. I fly with joy, filled with emptiness. "Threads" I have gathered from my experiences with photography, meditation, yoga, and the wilderness have created a "rope" that sustains me. The peace, serenity, and beauty inside me burst out.

I never believed in my beauty as a model, but here I am, 57 years old, with a double mastectomy, hair fried from radiation, never feeling more beautiful! It's another shift, front to back.

When I was a child, in my nightmares I used to fall into a black abyss. Now there are moments when I tumble inward, into my own body. I climb to the attic, my brain, and being who I am, compulsively start cleaning everything! I come upon a small trunk, unlock it and open it up. Inside, I find who I thought I was, who I was, and who I truly am. I was there the whole time, waiting to be released. I was there the whole time. I have gone inside out.

I now know that I don't have to conquer cancer today. I have come to terms with it. Brain cancer is no longer something to get over, it's an ongoing challenge, always present. It's something that's fallen in my lap. But has it really?

Lynn Kohlman

A VIEW FROM THE FRONT

The country girls—fresh-faced and innocent—are stealing the fashion scene with their milkmaid looks. Inspired by peasant costumes (craft and folk shops have the real ones), the new resort clothes are all dirndl skirts, small waists, aprons, babushkas and embroidery—a charming back-to-the farm movement.

Black voile blouse has smocking at the wrists, tucks into a white linen skirt with a smocked waistband. Sylvia de Gay for Country Set. $16 each. Third floor, Altman's. January. Peasant scarf, Greek Island.

Hoe-down dress of white-dotted shiny black cotton has its own white apron. Erica Elias for Charlie's Girls. $16. Third floor, Macy's. End of November. Paisley dust cap, Mr. John; button shoes, Capezio.

Country
Fresh
(Cont.)

g pink flowers on chrome-
llow wool challis give peasant
ok to a long-sleeved smock. By
ie Gladstone for Deebs. $90.
acy's Little Shop. Paisley-
nted babushka, Glentex.

It was the early seventies in London, the fashion place to be.
I had landed in the vortex of it all.
To be honest, I really was an overnight success.
Leonard, the famous hairdresser
who had given Twiggy her radical 'do,
decided a flattop crewcut would be just the thing for me.
Daniel, his hair colorist,
determined just how much
blond, green, or purple, at various times,
would be appropriate.

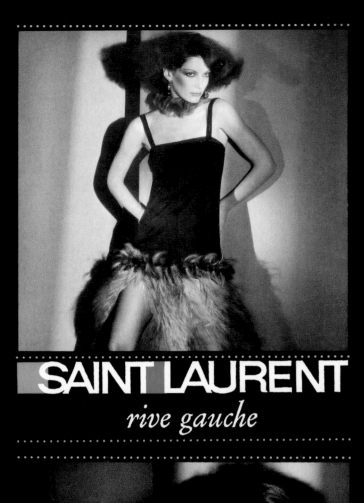

SAINT LAURENT
rive gauche

SAINT LAURENT
rive gauche

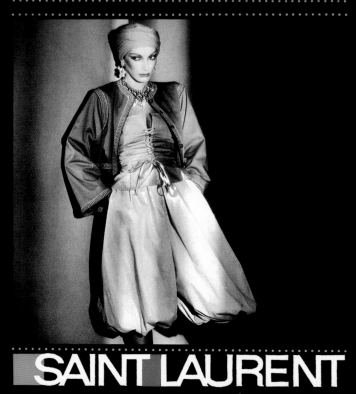

SAINT LAURENT
rive gauche

Back in the sixties,
there was no such thing as makeup artists and hairstylists.
As a model, you were expected to bring your own supplies
and get yourself ready for each shoot.
Unfortunately, nobody had informed me of this.
On my very first shoot, which was for *Mademoiselle,*
I arrived at the photo studio
and was directed to the makeup room.
I sat down and waited,
and eventually the fashion director from the magazine came in.
"Why aren't you made up?" she cried.
"I don't have any makeup," I replied.
"I've never worn makeup in my life!"
She stormed out, totally furious,
and returned moments later with a pile of drugstore cosmetics,
which she slammed down on the table.
I didn't have a clue what to do with them.
As you can see, by the seventies in London, everything had changed.
Makeup artists and hairdressers were now
mandatory at all photo shoots.

FAR LEFT. Pale amber linen knit
self-patterned jumper and dazzle knit
maxi skirt, matching hat,
in pink, yellow, green, purple;
jumper £25, skirt £55, hat £12, at Browns,
27 South Molton St, W1.
18ct gold and lapis bead bracelet,
£42; gold and coral double snake ring, £130;
gold and amethyst snake rings,
£110, £120; Cartier, 175/6 New Bond St, W1.
NEAR LEFT. Silky synthetic pleated skirt
and top, streaked and rippled with amber,
red, yellow, black, and matching cap;
suit £40, cap £6; maroon suède belt £6;
all by Missoni, at Browns.
Red one-size tights; Mary Quant, 10s (50p),
Selfridges, W1.
Dark red leather T-strap shoes;
Pedro Garcia, to order at Jack Hinton,
22 Old Bond St, W1.
18ct gold bangles, £105 each;
gold identity bracelet, £48;
gold and coral rings
from a selection; Cartier.

Lynn Kohlman

BEHIND THE LENS

It was a Sunday in 1982
when this portrait of Perry Ellis was taken.
We were on Water Island in his bay house.
Perry was reading the *Times*—I can still see and hear it so
clearly—when I said, "Put the paper down for a moment."
SNAP!
I knew this one frame had captured Perry.
He used it as his press photo until his death in 1986.

One night very recently,
I had a dream
in which Perry appeared at my door wearing his "uniform":
blue oxford shirt and chinos.
I got up and we hugged each other
with so much love and compassion

Perry, I miss you so.

Photography.
My timid nature dissipates, as I peer through my lens,
making direct eye contact with my subject.
The clicks of my Nikon become smoother and smoother
disappearing quietly into my breath.
My subject and I then start to "dance" with our eyes interlocked,
as I move slowly from side to side,
up and down, like doing Tai Chi.
Focusing so completely, everything becomes silent and peaceful,
until it is impossible to separate the observer and the observed.
This intense sensation cuts to my core, and I feel joy,
elation, and lightness; like flying.
This experience is so explosive that,
when faced with cancer,
I knew that accessing this place within me
would give me the strength to fight for my life.

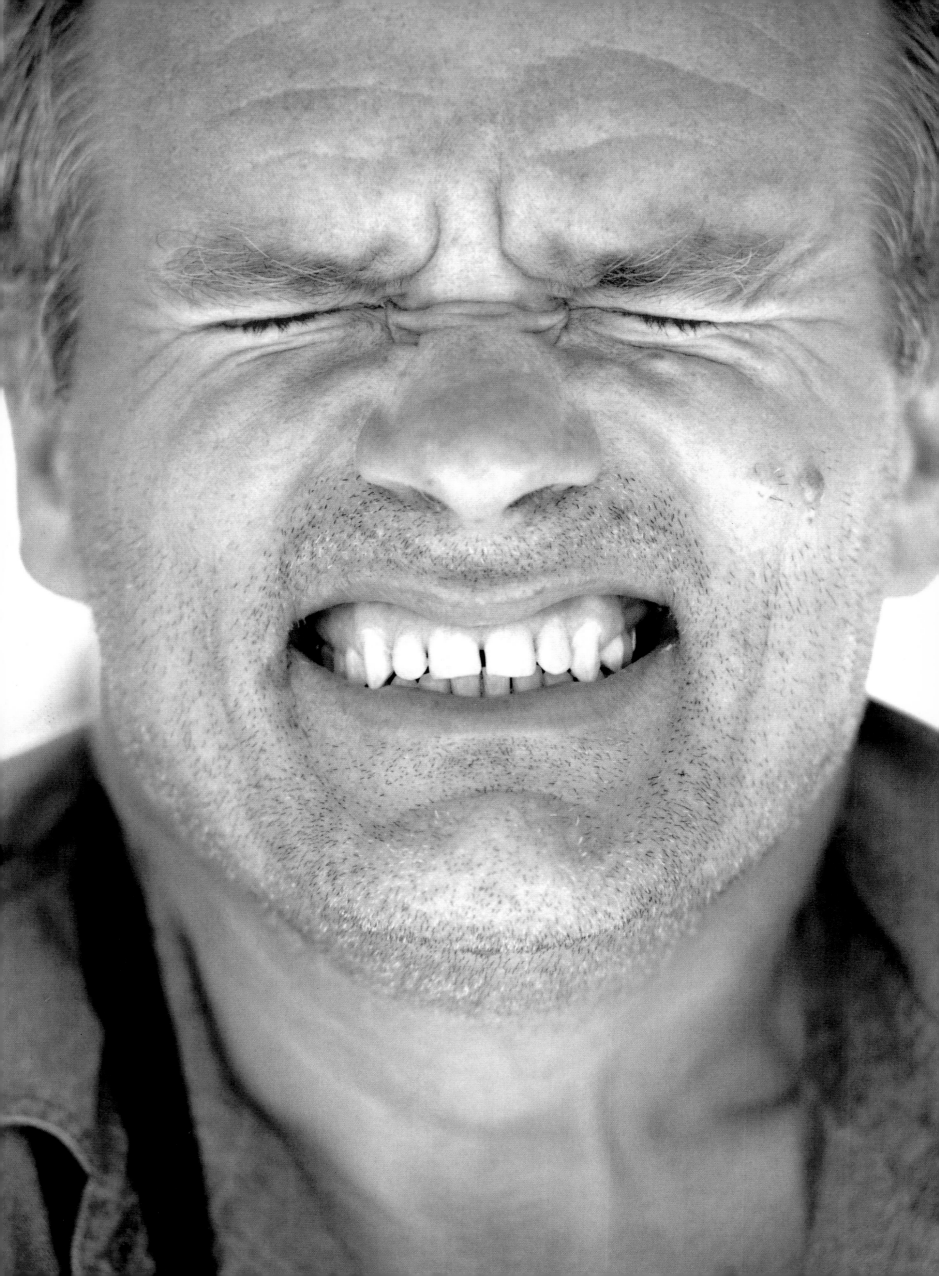

When I have my camera in hand,
I experience my own private space
where I go when I am creating, where I disappear.
I had never before been allowed to enter
this "secret garden" of another person
until I worked with Donna Karan.

With the arrival of the season's fabrics,
the design room became Donna's sacred place.
With a model facing a 3-way mirror,
Donna would pick up a bolt of fabric,
stand behind her, a little to her left,
look over the model's shoulder,
use her extraordinary artist's hands,
as the process of wrapping and twisting the fabric began.
Donna's head would tilt to the left,
and I sensed that I was seeing her mind, body, and soul
drop into where her creativity resided,
where quiet and solitude fell over her like a shimmering veil.
At this moment, I felt as if I had witnessed the magic
of the fairy godmother as she transformed Cinderella
from rags to riches.

This is only one gift I received from Donna.
We have known each other since the '70s
and been through so much together—
birth, death, raising children, spiritual retreats, you name it.

When I was diagnosed with breast and then brain cancer
she made sure I was at Sloan-Kettering with their most
outstanding doctors, and sat through the meetings there
giving me any support I needed.
I would open my eyes after surgery and there she'd be,
bearing love and gifts, anything to assure my comforts.

I often can't wait to see her, so I can hear her latest
self-deprecating story.
She is a unique comedy act—my Lucille Ball, my Ab Fab,
her own sitcom.

Most of the time, I feel there isn't enough I can say
or do to repay her for all I have received and learned.
But then I realize that I have shared with her my greatest gift.
With camera in hand,
I have taken her into my "secret garden"
where all is quiet, peaceful, and white.
We dance together as I capture portraits of her,
Stephan, her family, and the milestones of her life.

I have this image of the two of us
sitting on the porch of an old peoples' home.
Next to each other in rocking chairs,
slowly we move back and forth.
She will have that sparkle in her eyes
as she looks at me, and I will say "STOP!"
She will hold still just for a moment
while I take the greatest portrait of her ever.

There is one thing I'm passionate about
when I am photographing another person:
I need to feel our connection,
to resonate with their heart and soul.
For me, it is all expressed in the eyes.
I know when I have that particular eye contact captured on film,
I have the photo.
Stephan Weiss and Donna have been such longtime,
great friends that it never takes long for any of us
to dive into this space together.

We were doing a photo for the launch of their first perfume.
Donna decided on the aroma of white lilies,
suede, and the back of Stephan's neck.
Much as I love them,
I have to be truthful and say,
even the thought of the combination is unappealing!

This didn't interfere with how happy I was
to have this rare opportunity to photograph
the two of them quietly and together.
I took them to my favorite spot in the Hamptons to photograph.
With towering dunes we would be alone
and they could snuggle into the deep, warm sand.
Dusk was approaching, and with it a magnificent light.
The waves were crashing on the beach,
and the smell of salt air was carried on a light sea breeze.

When I knew I had captured the two of them,
the natural peace of the time and place
made it so inspiring that it was impossible to stop.
I took some memorable photos of Donna,
but when I found a spot of perfect light
and had Stephan lay down in the sand, the magic happened.
A deep "Stephan-ness" bounced back and forth between us.
Little did I realize, at that time,
the significance of what had occurred on this one roll of film.

When Stephan passed away from lung cancer,
there it was:
one moment, that was the essence of Stephan as I knew him.

This image became Donna's gift from me to hold onto forever.

I know it's not unusual for a mother to be proud of her son, and so, I must confess, I'm not an unusual mother.

Given the talents that both my husband and I share as photographers, I wouldn't have been surprised if Sam had been born with one eye closed.

When Sam was 4 years old, we took him to the family farm in Illinois. Camera in hand, he took surprisingly sensitive, beautifully composed photos of the landscape. He chose to shoot from the center of a road where the corn on both sides seemed to go on forever, and the telephone poles merged. Of course, his angle was a bit limited!

With Sam turning 6, we began a summer ritual of whitewater rafting, a week or more of camping in the wilderness surrounded by family and friends. Sam was particularly focused on the functions of our guides, practicing and learning to row and all the other responsibilities attached to their job. There was one guide, Leon Werdinger, with whom Sam developed a unique relationship. Leon is a talented and published wilderness photographer. Leon would occasionally go on bivouacs into the wilds to take photos, now Sam went along. All his gear on his back, he waved goodbye, not to be seen again from dusk 'til dawn.

Sam was about to turn 15, when he became one of the youngest employees of the rafting company, OARS. It was obviously time for me to cut my strings with him. It was a difficult task for me, but at the same time, I was proud of his independent nature, his desire to confront challenges and dangers, and take on real responsibilities. Every summer since, Sam has rowed a 3,000-pound raft down the Main and Lower Salmon River in Idaho. He and the whitewater seekers shoot the class 4 rapids with abandon. Given all this, he still finds time to take out his camera and shoot inspiring photos of the landscape.

We lived in the shadows of the World Trade Center. This is where the depths of Sam's talents as a photographer emerged and blossomed. With his camera, he took to the streets of our neighborhood and chronicled the devastation and tragedy. His photos were published in magazines, he was interviewed and appeared on TV, and most gratifying to me as the proud mother, he was chosen to be in a gallery show representing young artists' responses to 9/11. From this exhibition, his work was selected to be displayed at the John F. Kennedy Center in Washington, DC.

Sam, with one eye closed, peering into the lens of his camera, has allowed me to be a witness to his vulnerable, sensitive self. He has the rare ability to cut deeply and record with clarity the horrors of 9/11, then travel to the wilderness that he loves so much, capturing the beauty that resonates everywhere.

Am I an unusual mother to be proud of her son? No, I don't think so. Sam, you are an unusual son.

There is so much about a person you can never know even if you love them. Lynn and I have shared the best years of our lives—twenty-one years together—but through it all, I never knew how Lynn would deal with real adversity. She had lived a charmed life in so many ways. Beautiful, intelligent, artistically talented, she had glided through fifty years largely unscathed, even triumphant. The life we made together was rich with family, remarkable friends, careers, and a wonderful son, Sam. But on September 18, 2002, Lynn began a siege of suffering and torment enough to last a lifetime. I'm sure the events have been chronicled elsewhere in this book but here they are in short order: she was diagnosed with breast cancer, her mother died, a double mastectomy, a life-threatening infection from infected breast implants, an operation that removed the implants, but also removed any hope of breast reconstruction, seizures, brain cancer, brain surgery to remove the tumor, two weeks later the tumor had grown back, radiation and chemotherapy. Lynn came home trembling, barely able to walk, speaking slowly, facing the prospect of death. She had one wish, to see our son Sam go to college.

I saw the depths of her fears. I would love Lynn no matter how she chose to face them. If she had given up, I would have understood. But the person who emerged in the face of suffering tapped into stores of strength, courage, determination and spiritual depth that I could only imagine were there. She is undefeated by her cancer. The reminders of her illness are always present, the pills, the too frequent visits to Sloan-Kettering, the fatigue but she is undaunted. Breast cancer and brain cancer, both so physically and mentally degrading, she has taken them on and confronted the consequences. She does nothing to conceal her flat chest. She did cry when she threw out all her bras, but an hour later she had a smile on her face. She laughed when people thought her shaved head with staples was a punk fashion statement. She spends hours and hours with doctors but only complains a little. She isn't shy about cutting a visit short with friends by announcing, "I've got to get to bed." She soldiers on and fights.

She sees her doctors, she meditates, she does yoga, she drinks her green juice, and she sees healers. She plots her future. She believes in her future. She is willing to suffer so she can have a future. The charmed life is gone, gliding through life is a memory, but life is good. Her message is hope.

She is my hero.

EINSTEIN ON THE BEACH

In 1985, Mark produced and directed
"Einstein on the Beach: The Changing Image of Opera"
for PBS's *Great Performances*.
I took this opportunity to travel to the Brooklyn Academy of Music
every day for weeks to photograph the rehearsals.
By the end of each day, the design and direction by Robert Wilson,
and the music and lyrics by Philip Glass had me hypnotized.
The last piece, "Knee Play 5," moved me particularly.
So much so that Mark and I used it as our wedding "theme."
Here is an excerpt from it:

"How much do you love me, John?" she asked.
He answered: "How much do I love you?
Count the stars in the sky.
Measure the waters of the oceans with a teaspoon.
Number the grains of sand on the seashore.
Impossible, you say.
Yes, and it is just as impossible for me to say how much I love you.
My love for you is higher than the heavens,
Deeper than Hades, and broader than the earth.
It has no limits, no bounds.
Everything must have an ending except my love for you."

On September 18, 2002, I had surgery on my right breast. A lumpectomy was performed, as well as three needle biopsies on my left breast. Shortly after this operation, I received a call from my brother, Jeff, that mom, who had been suffering from Alzheimer's, was rapidly failing. Before I flew to Atlanta, where Jeff resides and my mom was in a home, my breast surgeon revealed that all three growths on my left breast were also cancerous.

My oncologist called a meeting. I had a choice between a single and a double mastectomy. He looked me squarely in the eyes and said, "Before you make this decision, think how you feel about forgiveness and regret."

My mother passed away on October 7th. I had a double mastectomy on October 14th.

Dear Mom,

I have not been a very good daughter to you. I have judged you so badly most of my life. I have always wished never to be a wife nor a mother like you. The last day I had with you, the embraces and kisses were as much as I could do to express my love before it was too late. Mom, I forgive myself, and I have no regrets for who I am. I hope you can find it in your heart to do the same toward me. I hope you can find it in your heart to hold my hand.

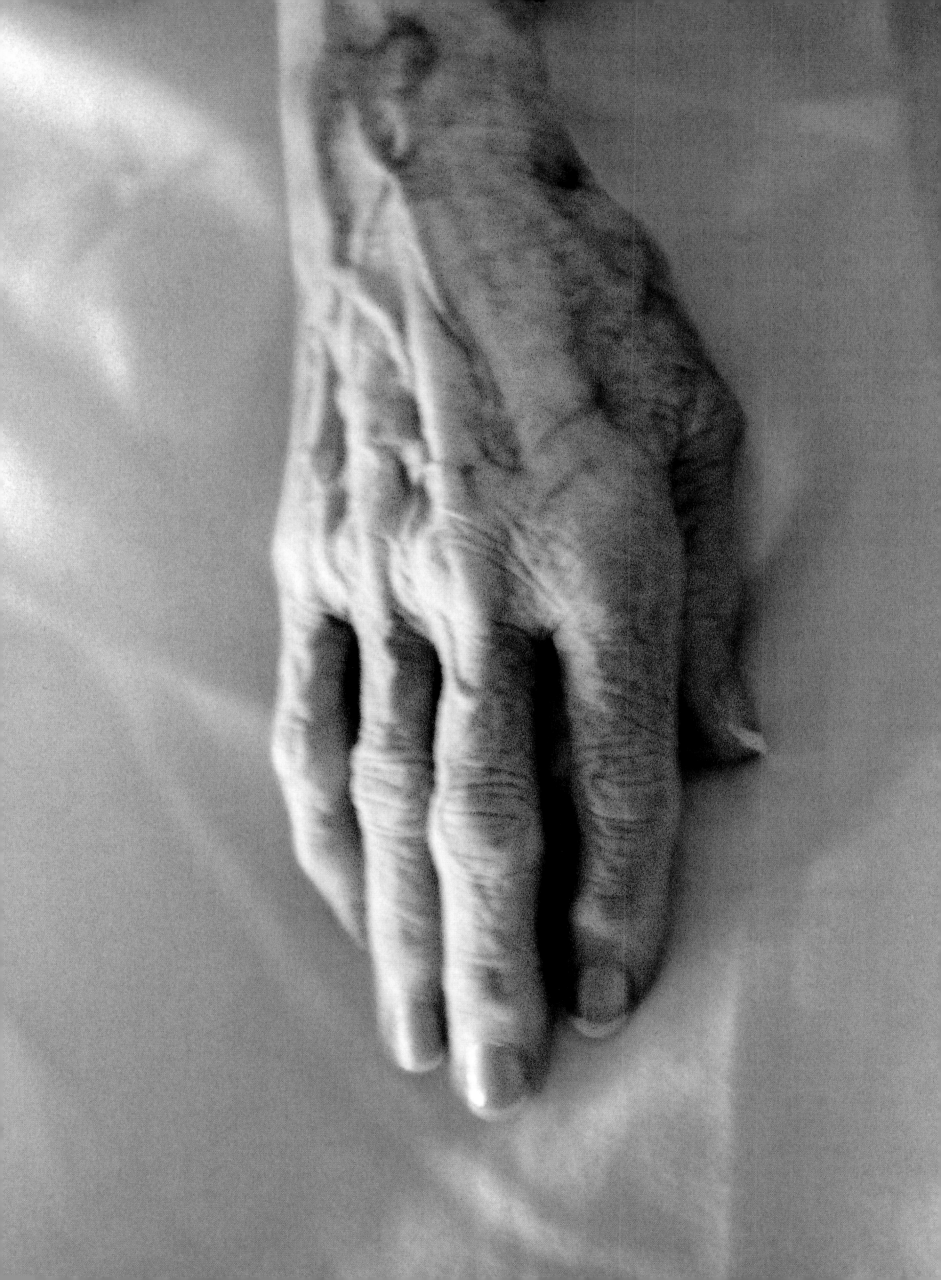

Om Gate Gate
Para Gate
Para Sam Gate
Bodhi Swaha
gone, gone,
way gone,
beyond gone,
awake
so be it

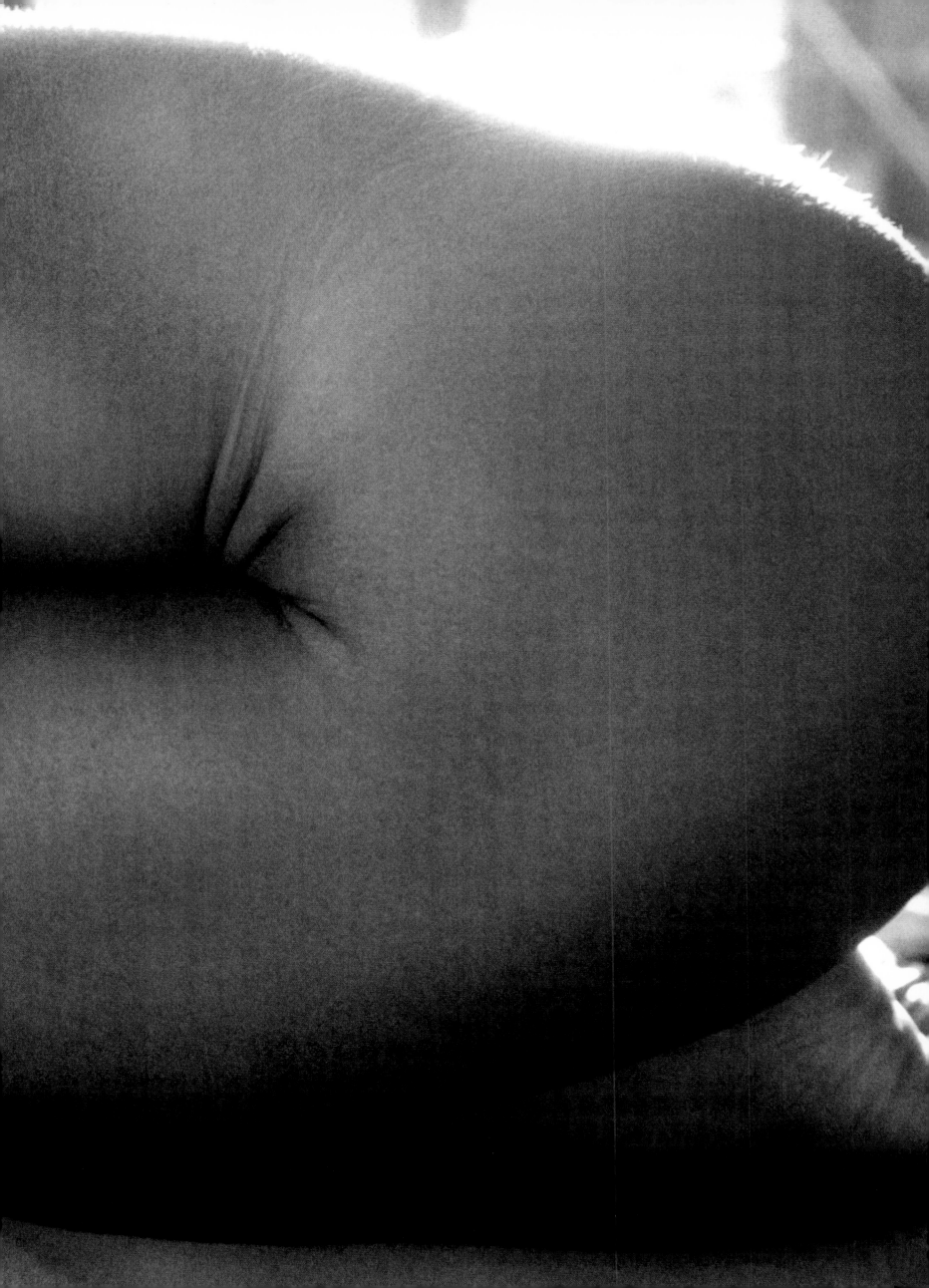

There is not a time when I go to my country house in East Hampton,
that I would miss the trek to Sag Harbor to be in Colleen Saidman's yoga class.
We haven't known each other very long, but it was love at first sight.
We must have recognized, even then, a rare connection and ability
to channel each other's thoughts and emotions.
Great teachers are few and far between.
I am lucky to have found Colleen.
With meditation and yoga, she guides me more deeply into my body and soul
than I ever thought possible.
In Colleen's classes, my body rhythms and breathing slow down
as I depart on my own personal journey.
My yoga mat turns into my magic carpet
as I hover above the ground like a bird
just above the waters of the bay.

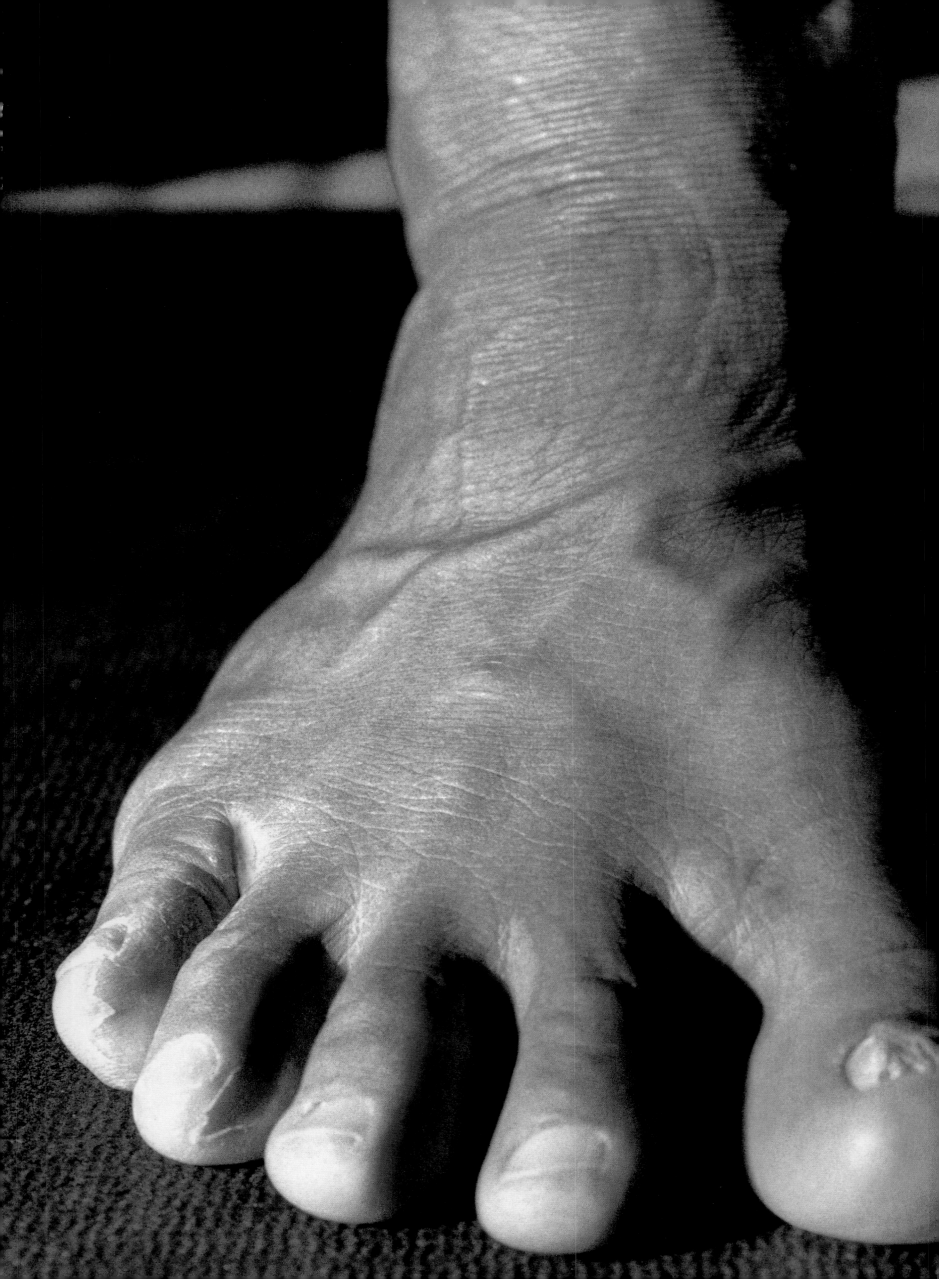

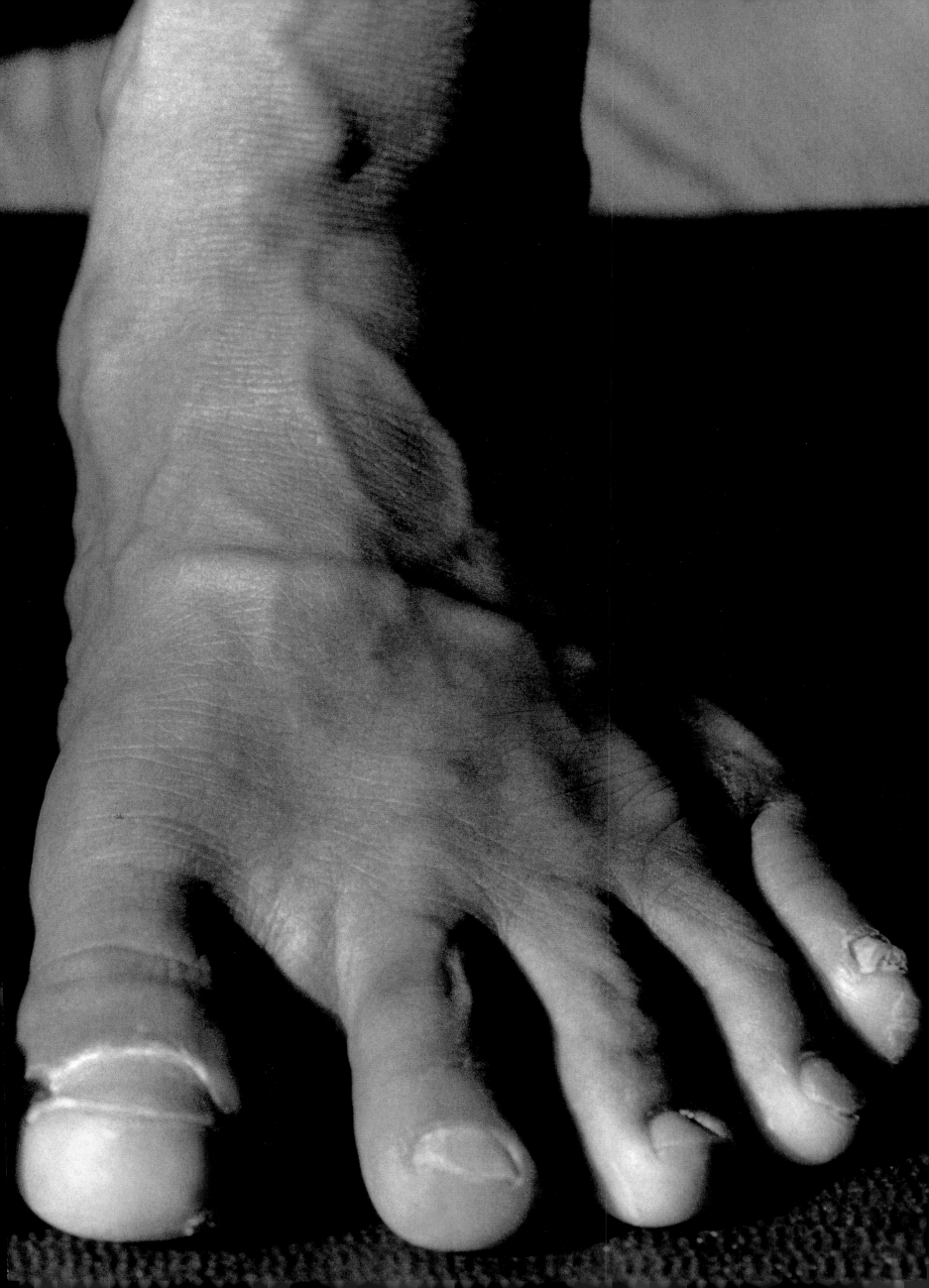

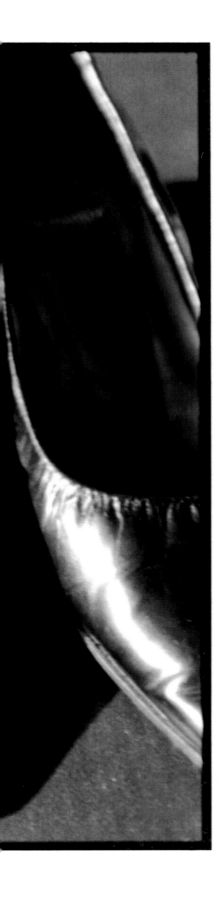

I rolled over in bed this morning
and there was
my perfect self-portrait.
I might have guessed—I'm such
a shoe fanatic.
Even I think of myself
as Imelda Marcos!
Most people, I believe,
dress in the morning by putting on
what they want to wear,
then select their shoes.
Me, I decide what shoe I'm into that day, many
times determined by the weather, then dress
from the shoe up.
There they were—two pairs of shoes,
a perfect expression of me:
the pointier-than-almost-possible shoes that
I wore with my jeans yesterday,
and my river shoes,
the Tevas, that I wore out last evening with my
chiffon dress.
I reached for my camera.

OUTER
SPIRIT

How to be happy cannot be taught in a classroom. Rafting through Idaho, the last place one might expect to find a New York City kid, I have found that the key to my happiness is in following the things that I have learned to love. This may seem simple and obvious, but I have met very few people who have put this belief into practice.

Sam, 17 years old.

For my 50th birthday, I gave myself a gift: rafting above the Arctic Circle with friends and family. This was the most extraordinary trip I've ever taken.

I couldn't even imagine what the landscape would hold for me. Hiking across the permafrost in the Arctic tundra and encountering musk ox was an experience unlike any in my life. I can only hope, for myself and others, that this pristine landscape is never destroyed.

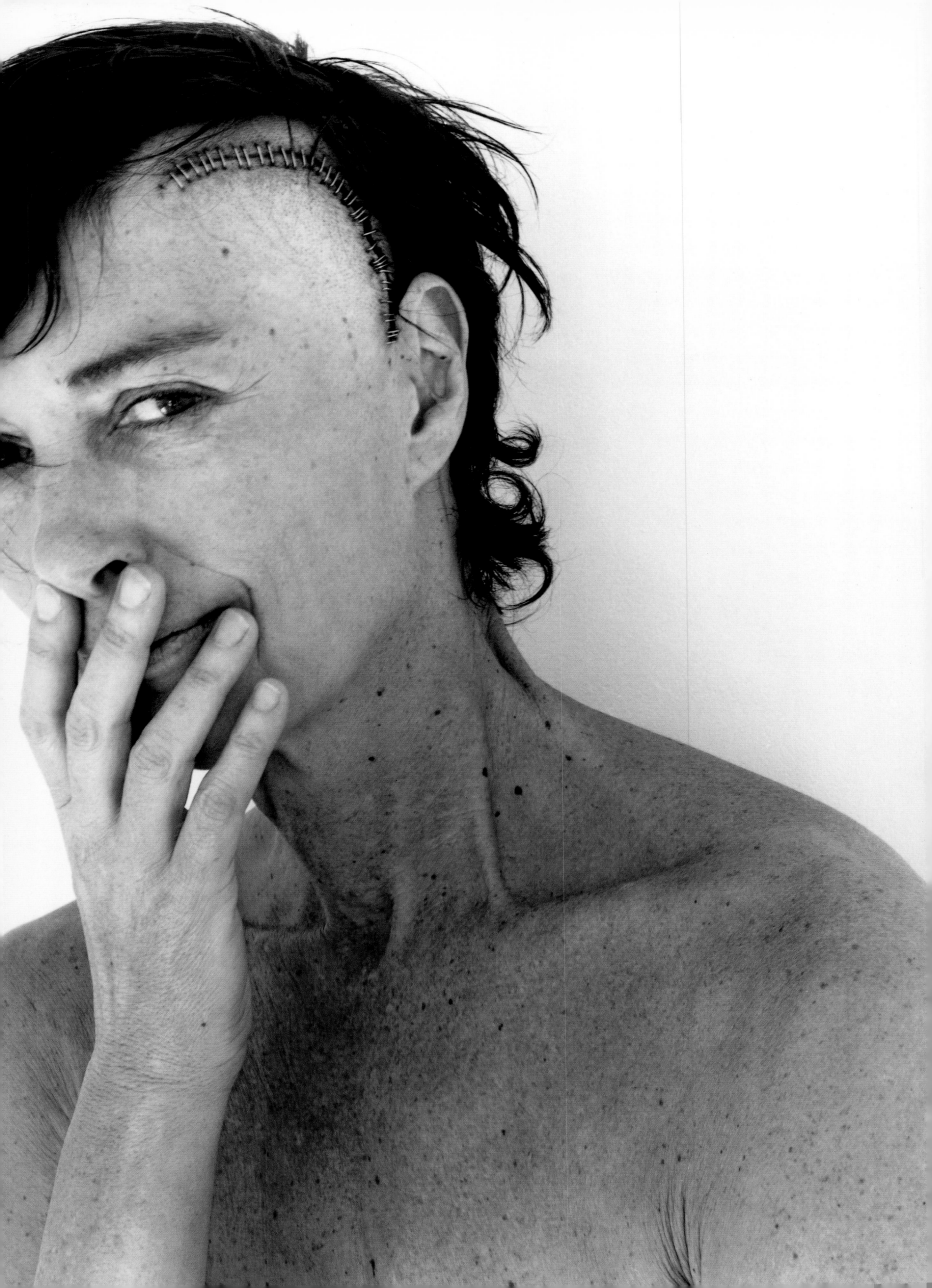

A WARRIOR SPIRIT

"Although I have been through all that I have,
I do not regret the many hardships I met,
because it was they who brought me to the place
I wished to reach.
Now all I have is this sword
and I give it to whoever wishes
to continue his pilgrimage.
I carry with me the marks and the scars of battles—
they are the witnesses of what I suffered
and the rewards of what I conquered."

"These are the beloved marks and scars
that will open the gates of Paradise to me.
There was a time
when I used to listen to tales of bravery.
There was a time
when I lived only because I needed to live.
But now
I live because I am a Warrior
and because I wish one day
to be in the company of Him
for whom I have fought so hard."

from *Warrior of the Light*
by Paulo Coelho

Δ

K 150

A. Narayana   00-037-998

Kohlman Lynn

Most people thought if you had it,
you were going to die,
and even if you survived the treatment,
it was inconceivable that
you didn't come out a cripple.
But I challenged that
assumption by returning to
a full, productive life.
I had behaved...as if death
was an option.

from *Every Second Counts*
by Lance Armstrong

I open my eyes in the hospital and there, around my bed, are relatives. I'm not talking about the local variety; I'm talking Atlanta, Chicago, and Brooklyn. Very nice, I think, for all of them to be here. My next thought, however, is something's wrong with this picture, especially since some of them have tears welling up in their eyes. Is there something I'm not getting here?

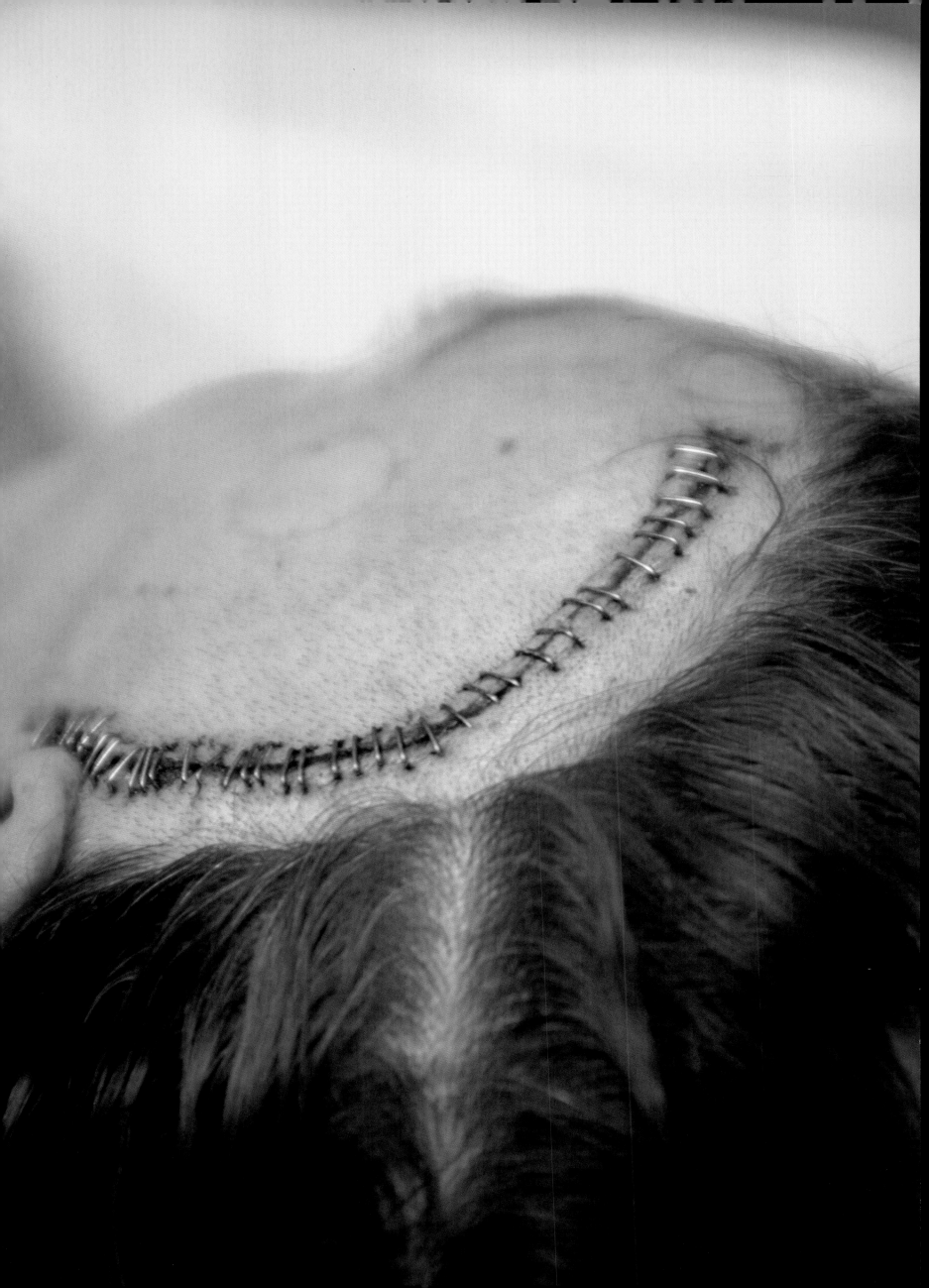

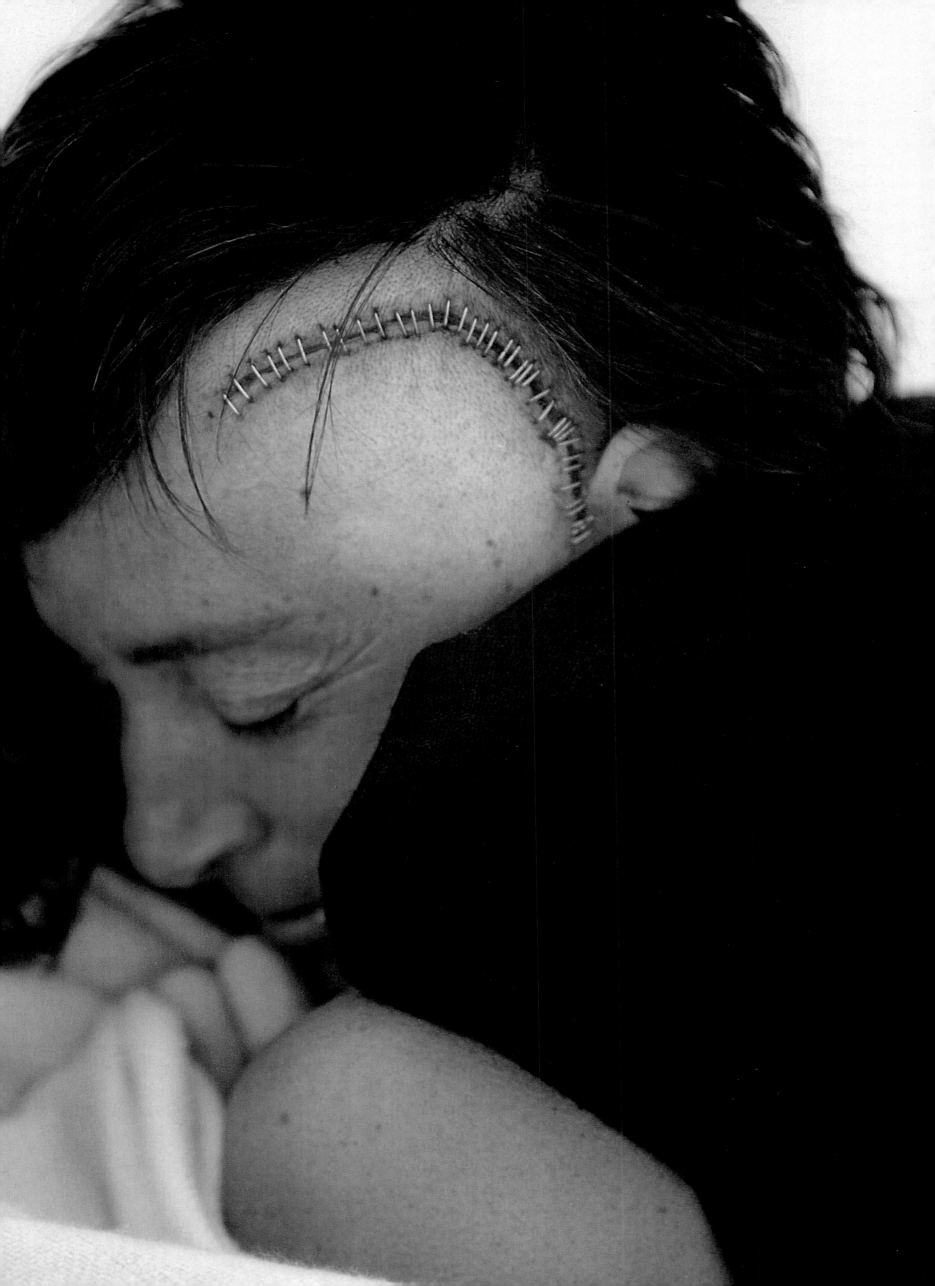

Dear Mom,

I must start with an apology; Dad was easy. You are quite the opposite and I could not think of a gift that would not end up on a hanger in the country or stored away in the depths of the basement. For now, this letter will have to stand as my gift to you. At a later date, when I find you are in need of a particular object, it will be purchased and given to you as my late, but not forgotten Christmas present.

I love you Mom. In the past five months I have seen you and my father like I have never seen the two of you before. When I came home to see you and Dad in the family meeting position, I was totally unprepared for what I was about to hear. When the words came from Dad's mouth I was devastated. Not only because I had just heard my mother has breast cancer, but also seeing the two of you looking as you did was hard to take at first. But Mom you are the most positive person I know and you always tell me to tough it out and that by toughing it out something positive will be gained by the experience.

That positive something is the strengthening of my relationship with you and with Dad, but most of all, our relationship with each other as a three person family unit. Despite the obvious, the last five months have been our best as a family. The bonds between the three of us were strong five months ago, but in the face of such adversity as we faced and continue to face, these strong bonds became stronger. Not only do I feel closer to you and Dad, but I also feel as if I became an equal member of the family.

This ordeal has been a great awakening for us as a family. It will be overcome and soon be put behind us, but it is important to take what we can from it. In a way it serves an important purpose, it brought us together like no vacation or other luxury of ours could.

To get back to the point, I love you Mom. Not only do I love you, but it is evident through the phone calls, letters, and visitors that I am only one of many. You are the absolute best mother a son could hope for, the best wife a husband could hope for (according to Dad), and from what I hear, you are also the best friend anyone could hope for. There may be no person on the face of this earth as loved as you, only I love you the most.

Sam, 16 years old
Christmas 2002

After my brain cancer was diagnosed,
my oncologist, Dr. Larry Norton, said,
"I would advise you to pick the five things
that you want to do and do them."
Then he paused.
"But don't even consider hitting the rapids!"

MY LIST OF 4 (I couldn't think of 5)

1. To travel to the wilderness and "hit the rapids"
   (not approved at this time by Dr. Norton)
2. To take a photograph every day
   (not too bad considering I'm writing a book)
3. To travel to turquoise waters and white sandy beaches
   (yes, thanks to Donna Karan)
4. To do a portrait of Neil Young
   (yes, if this tank top counts)

Little did I know that Neil
was going to appear at Madison Square Garden.
Donna, being Donna,
got VIP tickets to this inspiring performance of "Greendale."
Afterward, we were invited backstage.
That night, Neil autographed this tank top.
It took "a lotta love" to allow him to sign my Helmut Lang tank!
The photo of my tank top,
is as close as I've gotten to a portrait of Neil so far!

Donna and I left down a long passageway in the depths
of Madison Square Garden.
Neil proceeded in the opposite direction through the crowds.
I was approaching the exit doors when I heard footsteps
running towards me.
A hand grasped my shoulder.
I turned, and there was Neil.
He looked straight into my eyes and said,

"Have a great journey."

sing a song for freedom
sing a song for love
sing a song for depressed angels
falling from above

slammin' down a late night shot
the hero and the artist compared
goals and visions and afterthoughts
for the 21st century
but mostly came up with nothin'
so the truth was never learned
and the human race just kept rollin' on

rollin' through the fighting
rollin' through the religious wars
rollin' down the temple walls
and the church's exposed sores
rollin' through the fighting
the religious wars
mostly came up with nothin'

a little love and affection
in everything you do
will make the world a better place
with or without you

Neil Young

Excerpts from
"Falling from Above"
Greendale Album

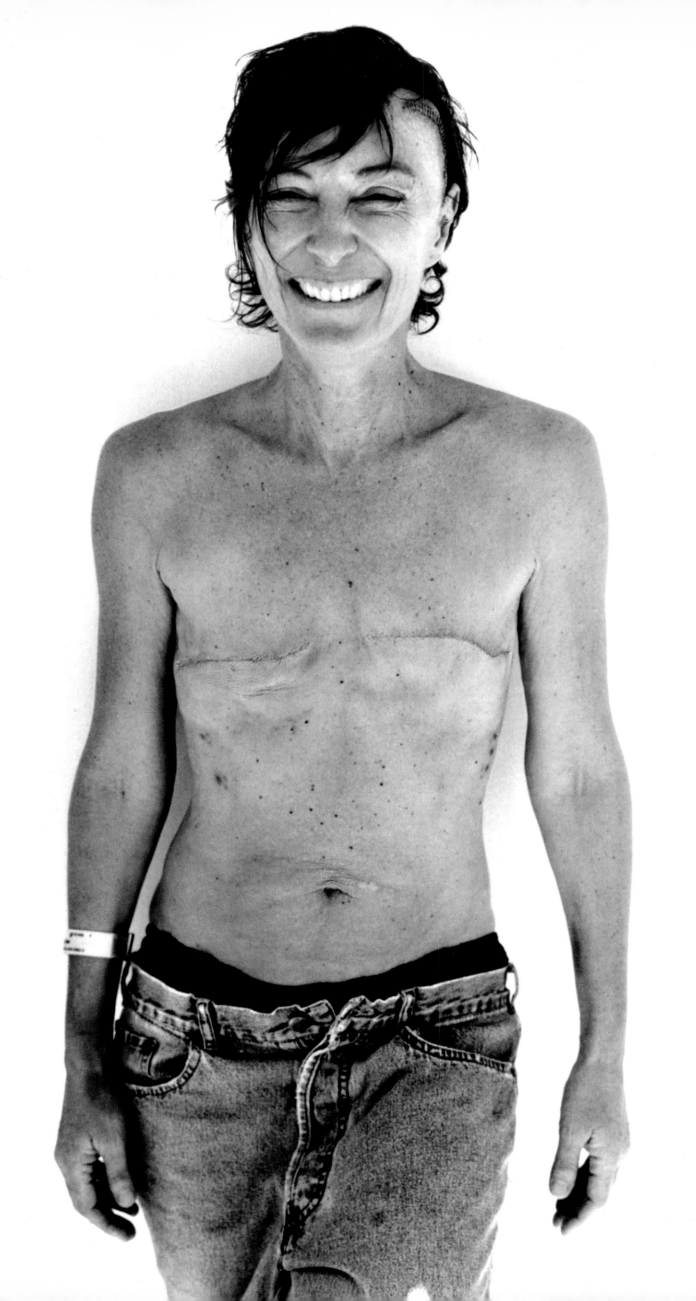

LOVING LETTERS
FROM FAMILY AND FRIENDS 2004

Coming Home

International woman
For years she circled the world
Living in Florence, London, Los Angeles
The camera followed her to shoots in Marrakech, St. Barts, the Yucatan

International woman
She was seen everywhere
Covers of *Vogue*, runways in Paris
Parties with David, Andy, Perry, Donna

International woman
She photographed the life
Pro football players. Fashion spreads
Wild rivers in the Rockies
Stephan at the end

But Lynn came home
She joined her life with ours
And wove a loving fabric
Of colleagues, friends, family, husband, son

Her light glows stronger now,
Encircling us, warming us, delighting us
We are so happy she is home

Richard Halverson

Lynn

The camera caught your beauty shimmering on glossy paper slim and sleek
Bold high fashion, elegance changed with a dress
A spectacular outfit, or sassy new look

Who was that person in front of the camera?
What image came close to who you really were?
Your eyes gave a glimmer of the warrior in the making

Years in between
Creating a family with Mark and Sam
Switching to the other side of the camera, showing the beauty reflected within
A lover of nature's design and gifts
Soaring mountains, swift rivers, glorious sky, canyons, and always people

Lightning struck with fury across your sky
Fighting, breathing, meditating, loving

Celebrating life

Helen Halverson

Dear Lynn,

How do we love you? Let us count the ways:

1. For looking over all the Obenhauses way back when and deciding that you would risk it anyway.
2. For having the generosity to include your future niece, Sarah, as a member of your wedding party so that to this day, a bouquet of red and pink roses, now dried, sits daintily on her bookshelf.
3. For giving us the gift of Sam—and for teaching him that "fusilli" is one of the first words that he should have at his command.
4. For tactfully pointing the way toward elegant taste in clothes and furniture for those of your relatives who love such things but aren't quite sure how to do it.
5. And most of all, for showing all of us what it means to live life to the fullest, day by day.

Love,
Connie and Arnold

Dear Lynn,

What a joy it is to hear you are writing a book. At first, I was amazed at your simply putting one foot in front of the other. But you have taken the existential to a truly praiseworthy level and are actually marching. Sousa would be stirred.

When I visited you last spring at the hospital, I expected overwhelming gloom. Your illness came on the heels of our parents' deaths, and I was tired of sick rooms. You, nonetheless, even if I've seen you look better, were vibrant. You were surrounded by Mark, Sam, and a group of friends who all seemed to greatly enjoy your and one another's company as if it were a fine party and not a hospital room. It is a testament to you that you had earned such treatment and it was infectious enough to dispel my guilt and fear of being there.

At your urging I spent the night with you and was proud to be the selected one. You actually slept through the night pretty well and didn't need much nursing. We did get a good opportunity to talk with no one else around, something we had not done for a long, long time. We've never been particularly close, and over the years most news of you was through Mom and Dad. This made you more a piece of fiction than a living, breathing person. Perhaps their passing even more than your illness gave me a great feeling of need to make up for all those years and really get to know you. You showed the same thing and even spoke of it more directly. Since then our conversations have been close rather than the previous formalities of birthday or holiday cards. I left the hospital room with a feeling that I, too, now shared and enjoyed that feeling of love I saw between you and your friends. And so, sickness be damned, good comes out when it's there to start with—L'Chaim.

You know, there was one other time I spent in a sick room with you. It was more than fifty years ago, when Dr. White wanted me to catch the mumps, or maybe it was you catching the measles. In any event we each have healthy children to show for his wisdom. However, once every fifty years is enough and let's have no more sick rooms.

I am sure that your book will help a larger audience march when simply walking is not enough.

Love,
Jeff Kohlman

My meeting Lynn Kohlman

I met Lynn Kohlman a few years before she met Mark and I really don't know what the date was, but I do remember her as a model gracing the pages of many magazines, ad campaigns, and the sides of a bus in NYC before we did meet. Then Lynn started taking photographs and I was the makeup artist on one of her assignments! We then had several location trips together where I got to meet her husband Mark and Sam (who was a baby), and that seemed to seal the deal of a long-lasting friendship. Lynn has a very detail-oriented creative eye while photographing and a keen love of natural light. We did a lot of work together and many pictures for magazines and ad campaigns to be proud of. The first thing I think you notice about Lynn is that she has a great sense of personal style...she would often inspire those of us around her without even knowing it. Time went by and we didn't see each other for years until I ran into her on the street in NYC in 2002. She told me about her son, Sam, and how she had suspected Lyme's disease in his knee and she seemed very upset with the long ordeal it was taking to get this out of his body. I told Lynn that I could offer some comfort because I had been practicing reiki and could help him. When I started my work on Sam, I began to get some very clear messages that Lynn needed to get a mammogram. So I called Lynn to tell her this information because it just seemed too important. I will never forget the phone call from Lynn that I received in early September 2002 telling me that she had breast cancer, then came the part of her discovering a brain tumor as well, and Lynn continued on with humor, courage, more chemo, craniosacral massages, diet, yoga, and exercise to beat this demon that has invaded her body. Every day has not been a picnic in the park, but I think Lynn is surrounded by tremendous love from her husband, Mark, her son, Sam, dear friends and family.

Love is the best healer.
Margaret Avery

I have a particularly lovely memory of you, that has remained clear and vivid over the years.
I came to visit you one afternoon, when you were living in London, at Linden Gardens.

A Mozart symphony was playing on the HiFi when I arrived, and we just sat quietly listening, not saying very much.

I became aware of this Mozart in a way that was totally new to me, and I realized that I was hearing the music with your ears; we were in the same spirit, the same "space," the space created by this wonderful music. And the music, Mozart's music, came across in these discrete moment-phrases, transcending the strictures of bar-lines and meter, becoming these living organic moments, which I had never heard before, even though I had been listening to Mozart all my life, and I know I was hearing this through your mind, your beautiful spirit, your way of hearing, and it was, and remains truly sublime.

I gained an understanding of how the human mind and spirit is elevated by great works of classical art, how deeply we can be touched by beauty, intelligence, truth, and compassion.

On that day, this was the sublime gift I received from you; thank you, Lynn.

With love,
Paul Buckmaster

Dear Lynn,

I just got a letter from Paul Buckmaster, and he told me of your troubles. I'm so sorry. I need
to bring you up-to-date to say what I have to tell you. For the last ten years, I have been working
as a Firefighter/ EMT, in Austin, Texas, when I wasn't touring. Because of my experience,
I understand the despair that can be felt in the circumstances that have befallen you.

In the time that I knew you, the one thing that stood out to me about you was that there was
always a great sense of joy in you, and I want you to know that it was not because of your youth,
or the ambience of the times we were living in, but was something deeply inherent in you, and
it is still there whether or not you can feel it. Please be aware that many people saw that in you,
now is the time to use it.

We wish you health, love, and clarity.
Shawn and Juliette Phillips

During a visit to Paris at the beginning of the seventies, a model agent invited me to dinner with some
of her protégés. It was the neck I remember most clearly, the back of your very long neck, a short bob,
and a wicked grin full of teeth.

Jonathan Weston

Before Lynn started as creative director for Tommy Hilfiger women's, I had heard we were
looking for someone and then I heard they found this woman named Lynn Kohlman, from DKNY,
who had a lot of experience.

To tell you the truth I was very excited about the idea of someone coming to the company that
I could learn from, but was hoping that she would like me and that I would like her! I was in my
office and heard that the new woman was in the design area and I went out to meet her and was
so relieved and excited. She had a healthy glow and inviting smile and when I looked in her eyes
we clicked; and I knew that she was a friend—mentor for life.

Lynn is such a good example of someone who is not only passionate in her career but as a wife,
mom, and in all of her interests, too—photography, gardening, yoga, etc.

Sometimes we would disagree, I wanted a certain coat in the show and she said,"Well, I would put
it in if it had more intention." Of course, she was right, but a little argument or disagreement here
or there would never dampen our relationship.

Last but not least, she had photos of older women in her office who had aged without plastic
surgery and they were all beautiful in their own unique way. All of them had great character
and their beauty from inside showed through. Someday, I knew one of them would be a photo
of Lynn taken 20 years from now.

Ginny Hilfiger

The first time I met Lynn was as a guide for her family's first river trip, a five-day float down the lower Salmon River in Idaho in 1994. Lynn and her family were a joy to be with—warm, engaged, positive people. On the second day of our trip, as we were floating down a quiet section of river, Lynn pulled out a disposable camera and started taking snapshots. I noticed that Lynn was holding the camera at a 45-degree angle, so I said, "Hey, Lynn, do you know you're holding the camera crooked?" In an unassuming way, Lynn replied, "Yeah, I know," and proceeded to snap the picture.

Years later, while at Lynn's home, I asked her if she could show me her photos. I saw several shots taken with the camera held at a 45-degree angle—the angle actually enhancing the shots. I was struck by Lynn's eye and creativity. The great impression though was of Lynn's humility. Lynn had excelled in so many fields and accomplished so much, yet, I've never heard her boast or brag. Lynn's quiet understated replies to my warnings that she was holding her camera crooked are a testament to what a wonderful and humble woman she is.

Leon Werdinger

Lynn has been part of our life for 28 years. There are hundreds of memories, so many things shared, so much unconditional love, filled with absolute trust. We have watched our dearest friend be brave and powerful in the face of a devastating illness and see her find strengths she didn't know existed, and humor in the places you least expect. Laughter is a great tool. It can help you through the worst scenario, and there is no predicting what Lynn will do or say.

Lynn is always suprising, just when you think you know everything about her, she will tell you some-thing about her that was really impressive, but somehow she forgot to mention until now. Probably because her life is so full of forward motion. Little did we know what was just a few weeks away.

Our families are joined at the hip. We've shared weddings, baby showers, births of children, deaths of parents. Vacations, parties, beach houses, etc. Lynn and Laura share the same birthday. Lynn loves celebrating her birthday on the river, and she is fearless. For years, Lynn, Mark, and Sam have gone whitewater rafting. Along with a dozen close friends and family, we joined them on an expedition to the wilds of British Columbia. The drop off by seaplane was a half-hour after the logging roads ended. We should have paid more attention to the word "expedition." The river was fast, furious, and terrifying. On the first day, a raft flipped at the top of a class 5 rapid, bodies went flying, and some were trapped under the raft. Lynn had been pushed under and when she finally surfaced, her body was trapped between the raft and a huge log. With some luck, all were rescued, but battered. It was how everyone handled the experience that was so impressive. Not only did we all finish the 10 day trip, but next summer Lynn talked everyone into another trip. This is how Lynn lives her life, no matter what she is given to deal with, she finds a way to survive and do it with dignity. She re-groups and goes forward. Fearless flying.

It is not really possible to catch the essence of Lynn on paper. She is so talented, so intelligent, and so very sexy. Through this huge ordeal with cancer, Lynn never lost that sensual quality and that remarkable allure she has, Just try to resist her smile. It's as natural to her as breathing. At the hospital, the doctors were all bumping into each other to see how she was doing. It seemed no matter what they had to remove from her body, it would not take away her spirit and her determination to heal herself. We are best of friends. In sickness and in health. We know Lynn is a gift from the gods. Her journey has made us all stronger, more complete, more blessed.

Laura and Bill Hudson

Echoing off the towering walls of the Grand Canyon or flowing over the tundra in the Arctic wilderness, through desert air so hot it burned your nostrils or carried above the calving glacier in a lake of ancient clear water—her laughter

In a pristine alpine meadow or in the stark reality of a cancer treatment room—her laughter

Around a river campfire or dining room table with friends and family in the rush of whitewater rapids or on the glassy still of a saltwater pond—her laughter

First, that short belt from the diaphragm to a series of waves rolling from the back corners of her mouth—her laughter

Through fire and ice, indescribable natural beauty or the frightful challenge of radical medicine—her laughter

Always there, daunted but never defeated, and unmistakably that of Lynn Kohlman, our loved one and fellow traveler

Steve A. Wilcox and J. Douglas Elmore

Lynn, an old patient of mine, reluctantly came to see me after being diagnosed with cancer at the insistence of Donna and Gabrielle Roth. She was afraid, confused, and frail. When Donna called from Parrot Cay a few weeks later to say Lynn was having these neurological problems down there, I thought this was the beginning of the end.

But, contrary to accepted wisdom, Lynn has fought the odds and is now growing stronger by the day. Her old spunky, witty, cheery, yet gracious and loving self has begun to reappear.

I attribute this less to the chemo and radiation and more to the intangibles; her will to live, her open heart, her belief in her own healing capacity, the love and support of her family, Donna and friends, the love, food, and nurturing of Jill, not to mention the healing music, yoga, and acupuncture. Her willingness to love and live is a constant reminder to all of us of what is truly important in life. I feel blessed to have her in my life.

Frank Lipman, M.D.

There's a photograph of you, just standing there, a smile is covering your face. You're nude and you're showing the burden you've obviously accepted in such a beautiful way. There is nothing I could admire more. You've agreed to live your destiny, karma, or however you would like to call it. To accept everything coming toward you is what enlightenment means to me. The moment I saw this photograph, I knew that you've gotten to this place, and I wish that one day I'll be able to get there as well.

Peter Lindbergh

Timid eyes
eyes like a doe
taken down like a jagged mirror
so many images
shattered and scattered
put in chronological order
by her dad

But who is she?
a collection of thoughts,
a collection of memories,
a collection of photographs,
some forgotten future.
A swipe of a samurai's sword
the length of an exhalation
Something's gone
way gone

So much force
so much turbulence
is fed into a single river
by so many tributaries.
Is there hope
that the waters will soothe and cleanse?
She sees beauty
intense beauty
and we see beauty reflected
in her eye.

Is there only love left in her
Is there only love in her
only love is in her
she is love
love is
love

Rodney Yee

Something About Lynn.

Lynn is a warrior, a goddess, and a damn stubborn Leo!!!! No one can tell her what to do or not to do. She has her own drummer and she dances to it with the most mischievous sparkle in her eyes.

Neither mastectomy nor brain surgery has kept her from missing a single 10:30 a.m. Sunday morning yoga class (the most challenging class on the schedule). I have strongly suggested that she miss a few, that I would come to her house and teach her some restorative poses. She twinkles, says OK, but then proceeds to take her place on the mat at 10:30 with 37 staples in her head. She lights up the room with the energy coursing through her beautiful body. And I play some Neil Young songs to try to give something back to her.

There is literally no stopping her. Lynn, in the 20 years I have known her, has never lived by anyone else's rules. She is not anesthetized. It will take more than cancer to dampen her fire. She is awake. She is love.

Colleen Saidman

I noticed Lynn before I met her. She was one of those very attractive women that stand out in a crowd and you wonder who they are, what they do. She had this allure and grace about her. Something about her shined above the other women in the room.

We were in a yoga class at Parrot Cay in the Turks and Caicos. Walking on the beach I met her. She looked so gorgeous and again, there was this allure and shine. We connected and exchanged numbers.

The next time I saw her was 10 months later and again it was in a yoga class. I didn't realize she had been diagnosed with cancer and had both breasts removed. The funny thing is, she is still one of those very attractive women that stand out in a crowd and you wonder who they are, what they do. She still had this allure and grace about her. Something about her still shined above the other women in the room. When we connected again we became fast, deep friends. How is it that Lynn has the time for a new person in her life? She already has plenty. I think it is because she might be the most open person I know. Open to new things, new people, and new situations. It is like she has all the time in the world to develop a friendship. To be present for a friendship. I am in the fashion business and part of what I have been trained to do over the years is to keep my radar out for the most interesting, the most talented, and the coolest people. The ones that shine above the rest. It only makes sense that my radar went straight to Lynn.

What amazes and fascinates me is even after having to go through all her intense medical stuff, she is by far the most attractive woman in a crowd and you still wonder who she is and what she does. She is even more alluring and graceful. Something about her shines even brighter. Lynn told me she found gold. I really think it is just Lynn finding more of Lynn.

Julie Gilhart

Witness

I've seen illness and pain, yet laughter and light
I've seen tears and fears for tears and plain fear
I have seen loneliness, I have seen love
Frustration, perseverance, success, empowerment
Truth and longing
Beauty and being beautiful
Enchanted and enchanting, caring and sharing
We've been shopping, fulfilling those needs
Generous and joyous stubborn yet determined
Perfection, there is music
Listening Yogini, Dakini
A spinner or storyteller
There is hunger
She's seen green has gone green
Live and living encompassing all life
Is Lynn

Jill Pettijohn

It is a common practice for my fellow spin instructors and me to sit around gossiping about the people who take our classes. There's the weird one in the front row, the woman singing at the top of her lungs and, of course, there is always someone who spins to a rhythm of their own making. Whenever my colleagues and I hash away at these sessions, there is sometimes a moment, a calm in the midst of our obnoxious debacle, when one of us might say, ahh, yes, but did you see the beautiful lady today? The "beautiful lady," the strong, calm, warmhearted woman who would glide effortlessly through a gut-wrenching forty-five minute spin class and leave the studio as refreshed, calm, and beautiful as when she entered.

There was something special about Lynn. There was something about her, besides her obviously breathtaking presence; there was something in her eyes. She was captivating.

She had contracted breast cancer and chances were very high that she was going to need to have her breasts removed. I wasn't worried. I knew Lynn would conquer it. One day, Lynn wanted to take class. Okay, I responded quickly. I was nervous yet excited at the same time. I was going to have the opportunity to see Lynn, to really confront this tumor and share some of my strength with her.

The day arrived, the studio was packed. I was aware that Lynn had been practicing yoga through-out the last month or so. I trusted her instincts to come back to class. All of a sudden, Lynn was standing in front of me at the desk.

I looked right in her eyes and felt as if our souls were intertwined. Yes, she was missing hair and her already-thin figure was now frail, but her eyes, the energy emitting from her looking directly into my eyes gave me chills even as I write this. It was electric. Life, raw energy, and clear light came shooting out of her, and the moment we grabbed one another, it came even more to life. I have never felt so alive before.

It was Lynn, the "beautiful lady," my female prototype, the perfect mother and wife in her purest form. Energy. It was incredible.

At that moment, I realized Lynn wasn't going anywhere. She was going to win the battle against cancer. A battle so many others had lost. She was going to be the Lance Armstrong within my arms reach. And I wanted to help her.

One of the greatest honors in my life has been the opportunity to instruct a class to Lynn while she was recovering. It is difficult to describe the sense of strength I achieved through Lynn's bravery. To look out at fifty people spinning at high intensity, exercising in a 70-degree room in the dead of summer with the music blaring and to catch a glimpse of Lynn with her eyes shut, surrounded by her troops just literally cycling through the illness was absolutely overwhelming. I couldn't help it but from that point on, anytime Lynn was in the class, the entire class was taught for her. To her. Any word out of my mouth was uttered for the sake of helping her find her way in the journey throughout her battle to save her own life.

What made Lynn's struggle so unique was that she welcomed help. She sought out love and positive energy. Never once did she seem afraid of people (and believe me, there are some scary folk in East Hampton during the summer). It was a lesson for me in truth and honesty. If you face everything head on, there is no denying what is happening and there is no backing down to fear.

Lynn had become one thousand times the woman I once viewed her as. She would no longer float up and down the stairs of the studio. She would march up those stairs with determination. Nothing was going to stop her from exercising out the demons that had infiltrated her head. At times, she seemed weak, tired, a little beaten down. At times I would get off my bike and walk around her space, a way for me to communicate to her that I was with her, holding her hand, by her side.

When Lynn asked me to write a piece regarding her recovery, it was truly one of the most rewarding moments in my life. I sat down to write this piece and the words just flowed out of my fingertips. It's been two months that I have been struggling with the conclusion. It wasn't until this moment that I finally realized why. This is an ongoing battle. For the rest of Lynn's life. She is going to be fighting this cancer. I hope to be by her side as often as she grabs my hand. Lynn looked at me recently and said, "I have been waiting for your letter." I looked straight into her eyes and said, "I'm sorry, I'm afraid." She looked back at me with her favorite Lynn expression, the smirk, and said, "AFRAID?"

Marion Roaman

The remarkable qualities of Lynn, her warmth and generosity, her creativity and wit, her indomitable spirit are all obvious to anyone lucky enough to know her. And undoubtedly these qualities have been alluded to already. But what is not as widely known about Lynn, what truly separates her from everyone else is the remarkable fact that Lynn is rarely, if ever, wrong about anything.

We were pointedly reminded of this a couple of summers ago when Lynn and husband, Mark, left a message on our answering machine saying that they were on the L.I.E. on their way out to East Hampton and would we like to meet for dinner? Unaware that they had neglected to turn off their car phone, the entire rest of our incoming message tape was nearly forty minutes! It was filled with a lively debate about who it was that had just farted in the Kohlman-Obenhaus airtight Audi.

Not including Charlie, the Jack Russell terrier, whose flatulence is distinctly recognizable, there were only three possible perpetrators, Mark, Lynn, and son, Sam. From Speouk to Yaphang to Manorville, the argument raged. Accusations and counter-accusations flew until, after a process of investigative deduction worthy of Scotland Yard, the finger of guilt pointed squarely at Lynn. After a long pause, Lynn flatly responded, "Moms don't fart." She said this as if it were an irrefutable law of Nature, the result of extensive research, a well-known fact. Anyone who knows Lynn knows how often this sort of calm and reasonable statement has ended a heated debate. Case closed.

Later that evening, over dinner at a local restaurant, Lynn asked how the book I was working on was coming. "I'm thinking of changing the title," I told her, "I'm thinking of *Moms Don't Fart.*"

While Mark looked stunned and bewildered by my remark, Lynn's eyes twinkled puckishly. She got it instantly, she always does.

David Feuer & Sharone Einhorn

PLATES

LYNN KOHLMAN

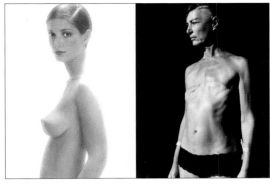

BARRY LATEGAN   MARK OBENHAUS

PHOTOGRAPHER UNKNOWN

PHOTOGRAPHER UNKNOWN

GÖSTA PETERSON

PHOTOGRAPHER UNKNOWN

BILL KING   PHOTOGRAPHER UNKNOWN

BARRY LATEGAN

GIAN PAOLO BARBIERI   FRANCOIS LAMY

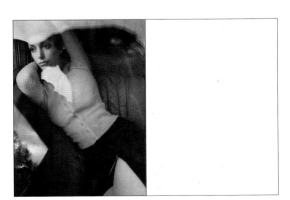

JEAN LOUP SIEFF

PHOTOGRAPHER UNKNOWN

PHOTOGRAPHER UNKNOWN

BARRY MCKINLEY

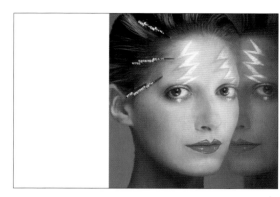

BARRY LATEGAN

GARRY GROSS

CHARLES TRACY

BEHIND THE LENS

FRAN LEBOWITZ
ALL PHOTOGRAPHS IN THIS SECTION BY LYNN KOHLMAN

PERRY ELLIS

KEITH RICHARDS & PATTI HANSEN

KEITH RICHARDS

JEFFREY BANKS

CALVIN KLEIN

PETER LINDBERGH

DONNA KARAN

GABBY KARAN & GIANPAOLO DEFELICE

STEPHAN WEISS

LYNN'S SON, SAM

LYNN'S HUSBAND, MARK

BEHIND THE SCENES

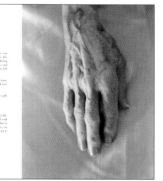

MY MOTHER'S HAND

RODNEY YEE

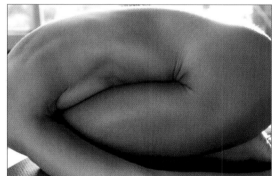

COLLEEN SAIDMAN

COLLEEN SAIDMAN

COLLEEN SAIDMAN

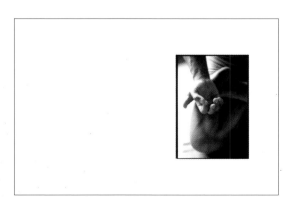

RODNEY YEE

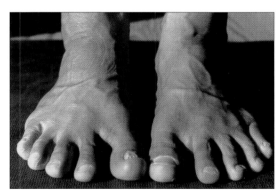

RODNEY YEE

SELF-PORTRAIT

OUTER
SPIRIT

THE FIRTH RIVER, YUKON TERRITORY, CANADA
ALL PHOTOGRAPHS IN THIS SECTION BY LYNN KOHLMAN

KNIGHTS INLET, B.C.

THE FIRTH RIVER, ARCTIC LANDSCAPE

BEAUFORT SEA

THE TATSHENSHENI RIVER, B.C.

BEAUFORT SEA

KLINAKLINI RIVER, B.C.

A WARRIOR
SPIRIT

PORTRAIT, ROBIN SAIDMAN

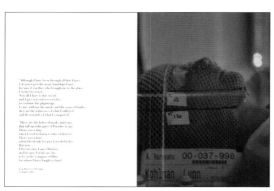

RADIATION, MARK OBENHAUS

SELF-PORTRAIT WITH EXPANDERS

STAPLES, MARK OBENHAUS

DONNA AND I, STEVEN SEBRING

DONNA AND I, STEVEN SEBRING

DONNA AND I, STEVEN SEBRING

FAMILY PORTRAIT: MARK, SAM, AND I, STEVEN SEBRING

MY TANK TOP AUTOGRAPHED BY NEIL YOUNG, LYNN KOHLMAN

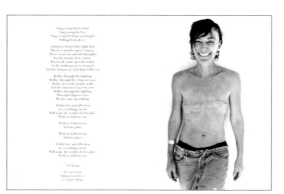

PORTRAIT, ROBIN SAIDMAN

INSPIRATION

Lance Armstrong & Neil Young

ACKNOWLEDGMENTS

First and foremost, Donna Karan. Without her giving and support on every level, this book would never have come about.

My friend, Margaret Avery, whose psychic powers saw trouble and strongly encouraged me to go immediately to a breast surgeon. Without this "insight" it would be impossible to imagine what might have been.

My "western" doctors at Memorial Sloan-Kettering Cancer Center, who treat me with such care and have aided in my current health. I have put my trust and loyalty in the capable hands of Dr. Larry Norton, oncologist; Dr. Alexandra Heerdt, breast surgeon; Dr. Eric Holland, brain surgeon; and Dr. Lisa DeAngelis, neurologist, as well as her assistant, Eileen Tiernan; and at Lenox Hill Hospital, Dr. George Beraka, plastic surgeon, who performed a superb job in removing my infected expanders.

My "eastern" practitioners who are leading me down a path to heal both mind and body. Dr. Frank Lipman, acupuncturist; Susan Brown, craniosacral therapist; Rodney Yee and Colleen Saidman, meditation and yoga; Jill Pettijohn, nutritionist; and Marion Roaman, who keeps me spinning as if I am a whirling dervish.

My publishers, those at Assouline, especially Susy Korb, who with her constant grin and cheerfulness, keeps me going regardless of deadlines (now I know why it's called that). My art director, Hans Dorsinville at Laird and Partners, who has been like a brother—we have frequent squabbles and quickly make up; Jessica Schlegel who worked with Hans, and pursued this project with such diligence; and Ryo, who came in to work with Hans to see the book through to completion.

My lawyer and advisor, David Bressman, who was always available to respond to my phone calls, answer my questions, and keep me calm with his judicious recommendations.

My editor, Linda Kahn, who picked up my "voice" so quickly and with only a couple of weeks before my deadline, was the perfect editor for me; Gabrielle Roth for her recommendation of Linda; to the photographers who generously donated their work; and to Harpers and Queen, Conde Nast, Hachette Filipacchi, and the Hearst Corporation.

My black and white printers at Lexington Labs, especially Jeffrey Kane, who have done such a spectacular job in printing my work throughout this book.

My life-long girlfriend, Laura Hudson, who is always there supporting all my needs, and to all my friends who reached out with prayers and love lifting me up and back to health.

My relatives Helen Halverson, a sister-in-law, who is like a sister to me, there in the hospital by my bed every time I opened my eyes; Jeff Kohlman, my brother, who flew in from Atlanta, and appeared at my bedside; and my aunt Joyce Kaplan, who opened doors that had been shut for too long.

My husband, Mark Obenhaus, who surrounds and embraces me with a love that "has no limits, no bounds," and my son, Sam, whom I adore beyond words.

Harpers
bazaar

DECEMBER 1969 5s.

PREDICTIONS
FOR THE
NEW
DECADE
what
the '70s
will
bring
IN FASHION
IN BEAUTY
IN PEOPLE
IN MORALS

Queen

25th JUNE - 8th JULY 1969 FORTNIGHTLY 4s

ELIZABETH DAVID ON SUMMER FOOLS
OIL IN THE SOUTH SEAS LOVE LETTER PRIZE
YOUR ORIENTAL HOROSCOPE

ELLE

LA DÉCHIRANTE
AFFAIRE
DESRAMAULT :
LA GRAND-MÈRE
PARLE

ÉTUDIÉ
ET MIS AU POINT

NOVEMBER 1969 2/

FLAIR
with fashion

ALL THE FURS
FROM FAKE TO FABULOUS

BIG BEAUTY COMPETITION
WIN
A WORLD CRUISE
FOR TWO